Children's
Guide to the Bible

Author : Robert Willoughby
Lecturer in New Testament Studies
London Bible College
Editors: Elrose Hunter
Leena Lane
Consultants: Mark and Louisa Willoughby
Design: Ian Butterworth

© text 1998 Robert Willoughby
© illustrations 1998 Tony Morris
First published in 1998 by
Scripture Union, 207 - 209 Queensway, Bletchley, Milton Keynes,
MK2 2EB, England

ISBN 1 85999 072 X

British Library Cataloguing-in-Publication Data.
A catalogue record of this book is available from the British Library.

Colour reproduction by Unifoto Pty. Ltd.
Printing by New Interlitho, Italy.

Children's
Guide to the Bible

Robert Willoughby

Illustrated by Tony Morris

Scripture Union

A note to the reader

The Bible is the most important book you will ever pick up. That's because it tells you about the most important person in the whole universe – God.

The Bible is exciting, challenging and a great help to everyone who wants to live life to the full.

The Bible is also a very big book and most people find they need a bit of help to understand it. That's what this book is all about.

I hope you find this book interesting and useful. Most of all I pray that it will help you to get to know God. Nothing could be better than that.

Here is a prayer you might like to use whenever you read the Bible:

"Dear God,
Thank you that you have given us the Bible, your Word.
Please help us to know you better through reading it,
and to serve you better through obeying it.
Amen."

How to use this book

This book will guide you through the Bible from Genesis to Revelation. You can start at the beginning and read a bit at a time until you reach the end. This will help you to see how God's great plan works out. Or you can look up the **index** at the back of the book for something you want to find out about. For example: if you want to know about the Ten Commandments, the index will tell you that you need to look at pages 36-37 and pages 38 and 40.

Have a Bible near you when you are reading this book so that you can look up and find out more when you see a Bible reference in **bold type** like this: **Look up Numbers chapter 21 verses 4 to 9 for a story about snakes.**

Where have we got to in the Bible?
At the top of each page you will find a heading which tells you whether you are in **The Old Testament** or **The New Testament.** It also tells you what kind of book we are looking at. Here is an example: ***The Old Testament* HISTORY.**

When did it all happen?
As you go through the book you will see a timeline at the top of some pages. Part of it will be coloured in to show when the events in this part of the book happened. And at the back of the book, on pages 110 to 112 you will find time charts which cover all of the Bible.

Looking back and looking forward
The pages with a timeline at the top are different from the other pages. They are a review of what has gone before or an overview of the next part of the book. It is as if you had gone up a hill to get a better view of what is going on around you.

Verses to remember
On some pages you will find an important Bible verse. See if you can learn these verses by heart and at the same time learn where they are found in the Bible.

Important words
Where you see a single word in **bold type** such as **covenant,** look up the list of **Important words in the Bible** on page 120 where it is explained.

Who's Who
At the back of the book on pages 118 and 119 you will find a list of the important people in the Bible, who they are and where to find them in this book.

Where did it all happen?
If you want to find out where the events in the Bible happened, look at the maps on pages 114 to 117.

How to find your way in the Bible
At the front of your Bible you will find a list of all the books and the number of the page where each starts. Each Bible book is divided into chapters and each chapter is divided into verses. If you see something written like this: **John 3:16** it means the book of John, chapter 3, verse 16.

Contents

Introduction:
The great plan

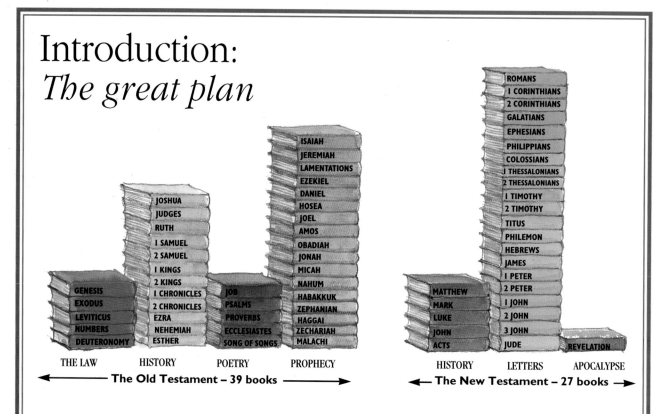

The Old Testament – 39 books

THE LAW: GENESIS, EXODUS, LEVITICUS, NUMBERS, DEUTERONOMY

HISTORY: JOSHUA, JUDGES, RUTH, 1 SAMUEL, 2 SAMUEL, 1 KINGS, 2 KINGS, 1 CHRONICLES, 2 CHRONICLES, EZRA, NEHEMIAH, ESTHER

POETRY: JOB, PSALMS, PROVERBS, ECCLESIASTES, SONG OF SONGS

PROPHECY: ISAIAH, JEREMIAH, LAMENTATIONS, EZEKIEL, DANIEL, HOSEA, JOEL, AMOS, OBADIAH, JONAH, MICAH, NAHUM, HABAKKUK, ZEPHANIAN, HAGGAI, ZECHARIAH, MALACHI

The New Testament – 27 books

HISTORY: MATTHEW, MARK, LUKE, JOHN, ACTS

LETTERS: ROMANS, 1 CORINTHIANS, 2 CORINTHIANS, GALATIANS, EPHESIANS, PHILIPPIANS, COLOSSIANS, 1 THESSALONIANS, 2 THESSALONIANS, 1 TIMOTHY, 2 TIMOTHY, TITUS, PHILEMON, HEBREWS, JAMES, 1 PETER, 2 PETER, 1 JOHN, 2 JOHN, 3 JOHN, JUDE

APOCALYPSE: REVELATION

The book about God

Who is God? And what is he like? Why should we even bother about such questions? Has he ever got in touch with us? What does he look like? How do we know anything about him? The Bible helps us to answer these questions. It's all about God and what he's like. It tells us what he has done, what his plans are and what he wants us to do.

How can we know God?

It is possible to know something about God by looking at the world about us. In one of his letters Paul writes:

"God's eternal power and character can't be seen. But from the beginning of creation, God has shown what these are like by all he has made." (Romans chapter 1, verse 20 CEV).

And Psalm 19, verses 1 to 4 also says that the world shows us God's greatness. (See the panel of Psalm 19 opposite.)

But by far the most important way that we can know the answers to these questions is through the Bible. Christians believe that God speaks through the Bible and tells us things about himself and how he wants us to live. (See the panel of Psalm 119 opposite.)

So what's the Bible like?

The Bible is not really one book but a collection of books. The first part is called the Old Testament, which tells us about how God chose the people of Israel. The second part is the New Testament, which tells us about Jesus and his first followers. Some of these books are long and others are very short. Some are history books, others are poetry. Some books are collections of laws, others are letters, and so on. In many ways the Bible is more like a library or a bookcase, filled with lots of different kinds of books. But all of these books are basically about one subject - God!

Learning about God from nature

"The heavens keep telling the wonders of God,
 and the skies declare what he has done.
Each day informs the following day;
 each night announces to the next.
They don't speak a word,
 and there is never the sound of a voice.
Yet their message reaches all the earth,
 and it travels around the world."

(Psalm 19, verses 1 to 4 CEV)

Learning about God from the Bible

"Your teachings are wonderful, and I respect them all.
Understanding your word brings light
 to the minds of ordinary people.
I honestly want to know everything you teach."

(Psalm 119, verses 129 to 131 CEV)

Who wrote it?

A great many people wrote the Bible. Sometimes we're not sure who wrote a certain part. It was written at different times over a period of well over a thousand years. Most of the writers were living in the land of Israel or very close to it. Look at page 107 for more about the writers.

What's the story in the Bible?

In the pages of the Bible we can read about a lot of different men and women. We also read about a whole nation, Israel, and how God chose their ancestor, Abraham, to be his friend.

Abraham's descendants became a great nation, called Israel, made up of twelve tribes. They also became slaves in Egypt and God called Moses to lead them out of Egypt to a land that he had promised them. Throughout many centuries the people of Israel struggled to obey God. He sent them messengers called prophets and other leaders to help them. But in the end God allowed foreign nations to conquer them and to take them to their own countries. This is called the Exile.

After seventy years in exile, the people of Israel returned to their own land and rebuilt the Temple in Jerusalem which had been destroyed. About four hundred years later, God sent his son, Jesus, to live a perfect life and to die upon the cross. God had spoken through creation and through his servants in the Old Testament. Now he spoke through his own son. For that reason Jesus has been called the Word of God. (See the passage opposite from John's gospel.)

The apostle Paul was one of many followers of Jesus who began to take the message about God and his son Jesus to the rest of the world. Today there are Christians all over the world. Christians believe that God will one day bring to an end what he began in creation. Jesus will return and God himself will be worshipped by everyone.

What's the Bible about?

As we have seen, the Bible is firstly about God. But it does tell us a great deal about many other very important questions. It tells us that human beings are important and not just like animals. Human beings are the highest point of God's creation and are his children in a special way.

The Bible tells us a great deal about why people do bad things and why there is so much suffering in the world. It tells us what God's answer to evil and suffering is. He sent Jesus to die on the cross so that people could have their sins forgiven and become friends with God. The Bible tells us how God sent Jesus to show us how much God loves us and wants us to know him. And it tells us how to live a good life that will please God.

If you want to find out how the Bible was written down and translated, look at pages 106 and 107.

Learning about God from his son, Jesus

"In the beginning was the one who is called the Word.
The Word was with God and was truly God.
    From the very beginning the Word was with God.
And with this Word, God created all things.
    Nothing was made without the Word...
The Word became a human being and lived here with us.
We saw his true glory,
    the glory of the only Son of the Father.
From him all the kindness and all the truth of God
        have come down to us."

(John chapter 1, verses 1 to 3, and 14 CEV)

BC										
2000	1900	1800	1700	1600	1500	1400	1300	1200	1100	1000

ABRAHAM, ISAAC, JACOB AND FAMILY

MOSES AND THE EXODUS   JOSHUA AND CONQUEST   DAVID AND SOLOMO

Genesis – *a book of beginnings*

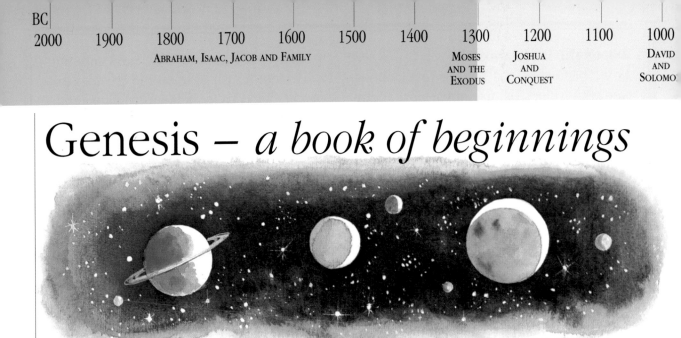

The beginning of the Bible

"Genesis" means "beginning". It is the first book of the Bible and it is all about beginnings. It is also the first book of the Pentateuch. "Pentateuch" means "five books", which are also called "the Law of Moses". Genesis itself is mostly stories and does not contain much law.

The rest of the Pentateuch (Exodus, Leviticus, Numbers and Deuteronomy) tells how God rescued the nation of Israel from slavery in Egypt, and led them through the desert where they received God's law at Mount Sinai.

The beginning of the universe

Genesis has two parts. In the first part, chapters 1 to 11, we read that God made the universe – the sky, the land, the sea, the planets and stars in outer space, animals, plants and human beings. We read that God was pleased with what he had made and made Adam and Eve responsible for his world. But Genesis also tells us how people disobeyed God and spoiled everything. God was very angry when he saw all the evil and violence. He was sorry that he had made human beings and destroyed all, except Noah's family, in a flood.

Abram begins to believe God

In the second part of Genesis, chapters 12 to 50, we find the story of the beginning of the nation of Israel, and how God began to choose them as a special people to be friends with him, to obey him and to serve him. We read about the first "fathers" of the people of Israel, sometimes called the "patriarchs". First of all, God called Abram, Sarai his wife and Lot his nephew, to leave their home in the city of Ur and go with all of their possessions to Canaan. At that time Canaanites lived in that country, but God promised Abram that it would be his one day. God also promised Abram that he would have a son and many grandchildren, great grandchildren and so on. The important thing about Abham is that he believed God. The New Testament often reminds us that Abram is the father of people who believe. Abram's story and how his name was changed to Abraham is on pages 22–23 and 30–31.

Abraham, Isaac and Jacob believed in one God. This was very unusual in their day. Most other people believed in several gods.

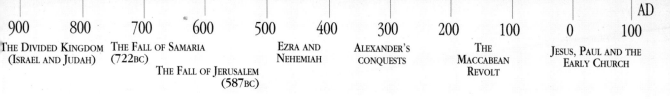

										AD
900	800	700	600	500	400	300	200	100	0	100

THE DIVIDED KINGDOM (ISRAEL AND JUDAH)

THE FALL OF SAMARIA (722BC)

THE FALL OF JERUSALEM (587BC)

EZRA AND NEHEMIAH

ALEXANDER'S CONQUESTS

THE MACCABEAN REVOLT

JESUS, PAUL AND THE EARLY CHURCH

The beginning of the nation of Israel

The people of Israel traced their history back to these famous and important men – Abraham, his son Isaac, and his grandson Jacob. In the Old Testament God is sometimes described as "the God of Abraham, Isaac and Jacob". God changed Jacob's name to "Israel", and that is where the people of Israel got their name from.

"Nomads" are people who live in tents and travel all the time from place to place to

find water and grazing for their flocks of sheep and goats. The country was very dry, so it was very important to know where there were places with wells and good grazing. Abraham, Isaac and Jacob were like nomads, but frequently settled down in one place for quite a long time. When the land was divided between Abraham and Lot, Lot chose the good grazing land **(see Genesis 13).** Wells often caused bitter quarrels **(see Genesis 26).**

Jacob (or "Israel") had twelve sons whose own children became the twelve

tribes of Israel. You can find their names on page 30 in Abraham's family tree. Genesis tells us how Jacob and his children had to leave Canaan and go to Egypt to find food. There they found that their brother, Joseph, was able to help them. This story is on page 28. So, Jacob and his sons settled in Egypt. In time they became slaves. The next book of the Bible, Exodus, tells how God rescued his people from Egypt through Moses. See pages 32–33 for more about the Exodus.

Facts!

In Ur, where Abram had come from, they worshipped Anu and Ishtar. Ishtar was a powerful god often seen standing on the back of an animal. In Canaan many people worshipped the nature god Baal, who was often pictured with lightning. In Egypt they worshipped Osiris, and Atum, who sometimes took the form of a snake, Isis. People believed these gods could make the crops grow and give them many children. They were very frightening. But Abram's God is all-powerful, all-knowing and completely good.

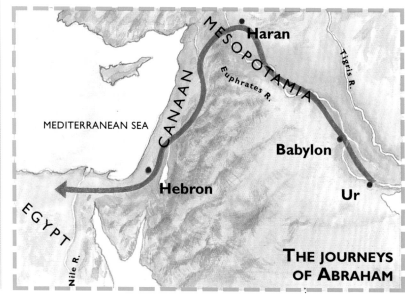

THE JOURNEYS OF ABRAHAM

Creation and the first family

Genesis 1-5

God makes the universe

Nothing existed before God made the whole universe. There is only one God and he is more powerful than anything we can ever imagine. He is also completely good. So when he made the universe, that was also good. Even mysterious parts of the universe like the sea, or the stars and planets, were made by God and are completely under his control.

God makes human beings

God also made human beings to be his friends. In the Garden of Eden, the first people, Adam and Eve, walked and talked with God, just as God had intended. God put them in charge of everything he had made. Adam and Eve worked in the garden and were responsible for it. Like God himself, they enjoyed seeing what they had done. God told them to have children and fill his world with people.

The sin of Adam and Eve

Adam and Eve were allowed to enjoy everything in the garden except the tree of the knowledge of good and evil. But a snake cleverly tricked them into doubting what God had said. They decided to disobey God and ate its fruit. Throughout the Bible disobeying God is called **sin,** and Adam and Eve could no longer be friends with God in the same way. They had to leave the Garden of Eden, and they had to work hard to grow enough food. Having children became painful. They had spoilt God's world.

Cain and Abel

Cain and Abel were two of Adam and Eve's children. They were brothers and should have loved each other. Sadly Cain became jealous of his brother, flew into a rage and killed him. He committed the first murder. **You can find their story in Genesis chapter 4, verses 1 to 16.** So right from the beginning of the world, people learnt how to disobey God and things went from bad to worse. But it was God's great plan, many years after this, to make it possible for people to be friends with him once again through Jesus.

THE GARDEN OF EDEN

We do not know where the Garden of Eden was, though some people think that it may have been in the country which is now called Iraq. It was certainly a very beautiful place with everything people could ever need. Best of all, Adam and Eve could meet God there. But once they had disobeyed God, he drove them out, and they could never return to Eden.

THE TREE OF THE KNOWLEDGE OF GOOD AND EVIL

God told Adam and Eve not to eat the fruit of this tree. Up to this point they had never known evil, though they understood the difference between right and wrong. The snake tempted them and they chose to disobey God. For the first time they had done something evil and found out that it ruined their friendship with him.

Did you know?

Many scientists believe that it took millions of years for the earth to become the way it is now. During this time, they tell us, life gradually developed. This is called the theory of evolution. The Bible is not a science text book and does not try to tell us in detail how these things happened. Instead it tells us truths about God, his world and the place of human beings in it.

A VERSE TO REMEMBER
"God saw all that he had made, and it was very good."
(Genesis chapter 1 verse 31 NIV)

The Flood

Genesis 6-10

God floods the earth

The story about the Garden of Eden tells us how Adam and Eve were the first people to disobey God. God became very angry because of all the sin in the world. He decided that he would flood the whole earth and destroy everything. Noah was the only good man that God could find in the world, so God told him to build a great boat out of cypress wood. This was called the ark, and Noah took his family and pairs of every creature into the boat with him. Noah also stored all kinds of food which would last through the flood.

The end of the flood

After forty days and nights, the flood stopped and Noah first sent out a raven, then a dove to see if it was safe to leave the boat. When the dove went out the second time, it returned with a fresh olive leaf and Noah knew it would soon be safe to leave the boat. God promised that he would never again destroy the earth with a flood. God made the rainbow as a sign of the covenant which he was making with Noah.

Did you know?

The ark was the size of a modern oil tanker (**look up Genesis 6, verses 15 and 16**). Several expeditions have claimed to find the remains of Noah's ark in Ararat in present-day Turkey.

NOAH'S SONS

Noah's sons were called Shem, Ham and Japheth. Genesis tells us that Shem was the father of all the Semitic peoples of the world, such as the Arabs and Jews. Ham was the father of the black African nations and Japheth was the father of most of the people who live now in Europe and India.

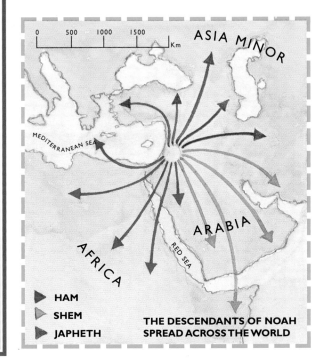

▶ HAM
▶ SHEM
▶ JAPHETH

THE DESCENDANTS OF NOAH SPREAD ACROSS THE WORLD

Facts!

Rainbows appear in the sky when it has been raining! You may see one if you look at the rain with the sun behind you. There is a spectrum of colours from red at one end to violet at the other.

THE COVENANT OF THE RAINBOW

From the beginning of time, God has made **covenants** with people. These are agreements which God commits himself to. He even began with Adam and Eve **(look up Genesis 2 verses 16 and 17)**. God made a new **covenant** with Noah **(look up Genesis chapter 6 verse 18)**.

A VERSE TO REMEMBER

"[God said] When the rainbow appears in the clouds, I will see it and remember the everlasting covenant between me and all living beings on earth."
(Genesis chapter 9, verse 16 GNB)

ZIGGURATS

"Ziggurat" is the name given to very high towers which people built in those days. Remains of ziggurats have been discovered in the Middle East. They thought that they would get closer to God by being higher up  and nearer heaven. The Bible teaches that we cannot get to know God by our efforts, but only by believing and obeying his word.

The Tower of Babel

Genesis 11

A tower to heaven

The sad thing is that things got worse again. People were very proud and began to think that they could somehow reach God by building a city with a great tower, called a ziggurat, to reach heaven. This is the first time that people gathered together to disobey God. So God decided to make it very difficult for people to understand each other and they began to speak different languages. This stopped them from being able to finish building. They called the city Babel and later it became known as **Babylon**, which sounds like the Hebrew for "mixed up".

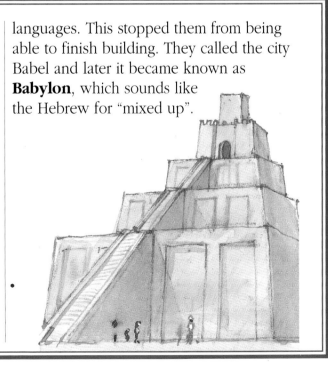

Abraham the father of nations

Genesis 12-25

In Abraham's time many houses in Ur were two storeys high and had as many as fourteen rooms round a central paved court.

Abram arrives in Canaan

Abram and his wife, Sarai, were very rich and lived in a wealthy city called Ur, which was in the country called Iraq today. Abram and Sarai went with his nephew, Lot, and his father Terah, to live in Haran. One day, when Abram was seventy-five years old, God told him to leave Haran and go wherever God told him. God said to Abram,

"Leave your country, your people and your father's household and go to the land I will show you. I will make you into a great nation and I will bless you; I will make your name great, and you will be a **blessing**. I will bless those who bless you, and whoever curses you I will curse; and all peoples on earth will be blessed through you."

(Genesis chapter 12, verses 1-3 NIV)

When they arrived in Canaan, which was the name of the **Promised Land** in those days, Abram divided up the land with his nephew Lot. Lot chose the land near the cities of Sodom and Gomorrah. Abram became more and more wealthy and influential, owning many flocks and herds. He was greatly respected by other kings in Canaan. God made many promises to Abram about the land and about his descendants. **Read about them in Genesis chapter 13, verses 14 to 17 and Genesis chapter 15, verse 5.**

LIFE IN A TENT

Travelling people, like Abraham, lived in tents. They camped wherever there was pasture and fresh water for their animals. Sometimes they stayed for a long time until the animals needed fresh pasture. Everything was carried on donkeys and camels. Whole families including servants, old people, women and children lived together in tents made out of animal skins and some decorated cloth. These tents provided protection against the sun, sand and wind.

HOSPITALITY

Many people were travellers and depended on the kindness of others to provide food and shelter for the night. Generosity to strangers was very important. This is called hospitality. It was thought to be a great shame not to offer hospitality or for anything unpleasant to happen to your guests. **Look up Genesis chapter 18, verses 1-8 for a story about Abraham and three mysterious guests.**

SODOM AND GOMORRAH

The people of the cities of Sodom and Gomorrah were well known for their very evil behaviour and God decided to destroy them. Lot lived in Sodom but left the city just before God destroyed it. **You can find the story in Genesis chapter 19, verses 12 to 29.**

God promises Abram a son

God had also promised Abram and Sarai a son. But, because they waited so long, Abram and Sarai began to doubt God, and Abram slept with Sarai's servant Hagar. This practice was quite acceptable in those days. Hagar had a son called Ishmael. God appeared to Abram again and reminded him that his promise would be made to Sarai's son, not Hagar's. At the same time he changed their names to Abraham and Sarah.

God tests Abraham

An even greater test was to come. In those days, people used to take their most precious things and offer them to God. Frequently this meant killing an animal and it was called making a **sacrifice.** God told Abraham to take Isaac and sacrifice him on a mountain in a land called Moriah. This was most unusual but Abraham obeyed and set off with Isaac. Thankfully God stopped him at the last moment and Abraham sacrificed a ram instead of Isaac. Abraham had shown that he trusted God.

Did you know?

As we have seen on page 21, God often confirms his promises with a **covenant.** For Abraham, and for the Jews ever since, the sign of God's covenant with him was to have a small piece of loose skin of a boy's penis cut off on the eighth day after his birth. This is called circumcision and Isaac was the first boy ever to be circumcised.

Jacob and Esau

Genesis 24-28

Isaac marries Rebekah

Abraham believed that Isaac was the son who should inherit God's promise. So it was most important that Isaac should marry the right wife. Great care was taken to choose a girl from among Isaac's relatives. They found a girl called Rebekah, the daughter of Bethuel, Abraham's nephew. In those days marriages were always arranged by the parents. They would decide who was the most suitable person for their child to marry and then make an offer of something expensive like pieces of jewellery to the other child's parents. The children had no say in it at all!

Isaac's two sons

Isaac and Rebekah had two sons, Esau and Jacob. They were very different. Esau, the elder boy, was a tough, outdoor sort. Jacob, the younger boy, preferred to stay at home. The boys were great rivals. Isaac preferred Esau, but Jacob was his mother Rebekah's favourite. On one occasion Esau came in extremely hungry from hunting. Jacob gave him food in exchange for Esau's birthright as the elder son.

GOLD JEWELLERY

Jewellery, such as rings, necklaces or bracelets, was a sign of how wealthy a person was. Rebekah was given a gold nose-ring and two large golden bracelets by Abraham's servant. Rich people would wear a great deal of gold jewellery. It frequently had some religious significance.

FOOD

People ate the meat of animals like sheep and goats, which could travel around with them. They also ate vegetables and corn when they could find it. The stew which Jacob gave to Esau was of bread and lentils, whilst Rebekah and Jacob made a stew of goat's meat for Isaac. We would find their food very dull since there was little variety.

Famine in the land

There was famine in Canaan. People became very hungry. It was very tempting for Isaac to take his family to Egypt where there was more food. But God reminded Isaac of his promises to Abraham and told Isaac to remain in the land. So Isaac stayed and dug the wells again which his father Abraham had first dug. Local people had filled them in when Abraham died.

Isaac blesses his sons

When Isaac was very old and about to die, he wanted to pray for his sons and bless them. Isaac was now very blind. He called Esau and asked him to prepare his favourite food before he blessed him and appointed him to take over as head of the family. But Rebekah helped Jacob to trick his father, Isaac, by helping him to cook Isaac his favourite food and by dressing Jacob up to feel like Esau. Although Isaac was confused, he mistakenly blessed Jacob instead of Esau. Esau was very angry and Jacob had to leave home quickly.

Did you know?

The first and eldest son (like Esau) was expected to take over, or inherit, everything from his father. This was called his birthright. Esau did not think his birthright was very important and gave it to Jacob. An old man might bless his son. This means that he would pray for him and possibly lay hands on him as a sign of passing on their responsibilities and possessions. Sometimes they would deliver a message from God about the person and their future.

Facts!

Rebekah would have ridden the 400 miles on a one-humped Arabian camel. They have feet like cushions and can walk across sand and sharp pebbles with little difficulty. Their deep-set eyes with long lashes and their nostrils close up to keep the sand out. Their thick coats keep them warm in the cold desert nights and they can even eat the tough thorns and thistles found in the desert. Camels can carry heavy loads and their humps hold fat to keep them going for long periods of time. Even their droppings can be burnt on the fire!

Jacob and Rachel

Genesis 28-36

Jacob's dream at Bethel

As we have seen, Jacob was a trickster. He had made an enemy of his brother Esau and needed to keep out of his way. As he travelled north to his uncle Laban's home, he slept outside under the stars and had a dream of a ladder reaching up to heaven with angels on either side. In his dream God promised to be with him always and to bring him back to the land he had first promised to Abraham. So Jacob set up a stone pillar to remind everyone that God had met with him there. He called the place Bethel which means the house of God.

Jacob works for Laban

Jacob met up with his relatives by a well and for a time he worked for his uncle Laban as a shepherd. It was here that Jacob fell in love with Laban's younger daughter Rachel. Laban was also very crafty and tricked Jacob into marrying his elder daughter Leah first. Laban made Jacob work for seven years to marry Leah and seven years for Rachel. Leah bore Jacob six sons and Rachel two. His other four sons were born to his wives' servants, Bilhah and Zilpah.

Jacob meets up with Esau again

Jacob found a way of keeping the best and strongest sheep for himself and tricked his uncle Laban. Eventually Jacob went back home to Canaan, but was very afraid of his brother. He prepared to give Esau a present of sheep, goats, camels, cattle and donkeys. The night before he met Esau, Jacob wrestled with a man till daybreak and would not give in. Jacob's hip was put out of joint by the man and, from then on, he always limped. The man was a messenger from God. From now on Jacob's name was changed to Israel, which means "one who wrestles with God". From then on all his descendants were known as Israelites. When Jacob finally met Esau, his brother was very pleased to see him and there was no hatred between them.

POLYGAMY - MARRIAGE TO SEVERAL WIVES

At this time it was very important for people to have a lot of children, especially boys, to work and look after them when they were old. Women often died in childbirth. So, quite often, men had many wives to provide them with children. They also frequently took their wives' servants. This is called "polygamy" and had died out in Israel by the time of Jesus.

Did you know?

In those days people frequently put up stone pillars to mark a place where something very important had happened. From that time onwards everyone would remember what had happened there.

Facts!

In hot, dry countries wells are very important and jealously guarded. The survival of whole households depends on them for water. In Bible times they were places where people met, especially the women who drew water. Both Isaac and Jacob found their future wives at wells. Because they were so important, they often had interesting names like "Quarrel", "Enmity", "Freedom" and "Vow".
Look up the stories in Genesis chapters 24, 26 and 29.

FLOCKS AND WEALTH

Like his father and grandfather, Jacob became extremely wealthy. He did this by breeding flocks of sheep alongside other animals. Sheep provided meat and wool for clothing. They could also manage on the rather poor grass which was to be found in dry areas. Fat-tailed sheep store fat in their tails, so they are able to survive even longer when food is scarce.

A VERSE TO REMEMBER
"[God said to Jacob] Remember, I will be with you and protect you wherever you go, and I will bring you back to this land. I will not leave you until I have done all that I have promised you."
(Genesis chapter 28, verse 15 GNB)

Joseph and his brothers

Genesis 37-50

Jacob's favourite son

Abraham's grandson, Jacob, had twelve sons. Young Joseph was his favourite, so he gave him a beautiful coat. Not surprisingly his elder brothers were jealous and hated Joseph. Then Joseph dreamed that his brothers bowed down to him and treated him like a lord. They were furious and, when they had the chance, they sold him as a **slave** to passing traders. The traders took Joseph to Egypt.

Joseph is sold into slavery

In those days, slave owners could use their slaves to do any job they wanted. Some slaves managed to become very important. Joseph showed that he was very clever and became personal servant to Potiphar, an Egyptian official. He was put in charge of all his master's business until Potiphar's wife told lies about Joseph and he was thrown into prison.

From slave to leader

In prison God helped Joseph to explain dreams. Some time later, Pharaoh, the ruler of all Egypt, had a dream and sent for Joseph. Joseph explained what Pharaoh's dream meant. There were to be seven years of great harvests, followed by seven years when the crops just wouldn't grow. At once, Pharaoh put Joseph in charge of storing food for the years of shortage.

Joseph meets his brothers again

Famine and hunger were very common in those lands. If rain didn't come at the right time or insects such as locusts ate the crop, people would often die of hunger. Jacob and his family lived in Canaan, but they had to travel south to Egypt to buy food from Joseph's storehouses. At first Joseph's brothers had no idea that this important man, who was in charge of selling the food, could be their brother, Joseph. Once they knew, they were terrified, but Joseph persuaded them to stay in Egypt. He made sure that Jacob and his family were well looked after. Joseph could have been very angry with his brothers, but instead he believed that God had actually planned it this way, so that Joseph would one day be able to provide food for his family.

DREAMS

Like Daniel later on in the Bible, Joseph was able to understand people's dreams. In the Bible God sometimes uses dreams to show people what is going to happen either to themselves or to the country. **You can read the three stories about Joseph and dreams in Genesis chapter 37, verses 5–11; chapter 40, verses 5–23 and chapter 41, verses 1–36.**

FAMILIES

Families were very important in those days. Children were expected to respect and obey their parents completely. Brothers and sisters were expected to look after each other. The family usually lived all together or not far away. Old people were respected for their age and were extremely important, as we see in the way Joseph treated his father, Jacob.

Facts!

In those days, Egypt was one of the richest and most powerful countries in the world. It was a place of learning and had libraries and a system of writing  called hieroglyphics. The great River Nile provided water for the crops which meant that people usually had enough food to eat. The river was also a very good way of travelling from north to south.

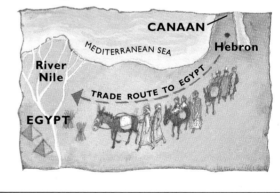

Did you know?

What kind of coat did Joseph really have? Certainly it might have been richly embroidered and very expensive, but the Bible does not call it "a coat of many colours"! It was very long and had unusually long sleeves which shows that Joseph was not expected to work with his hands. Usually it would be the eldest son who would have such a coat.

A VERSE TO REMEMBER
*"Joseph said to his brothers...
'Now do not be distressed and do not be angry with yourselves for selling me here, because it was to save lives that God sent me ahead of you.'"*
(Genesis chapter 45, verse 5 NIV)

Abraham's family tree

Genesis 25-36

Abraham's family tree
God had made his promise to Abraham and to his descendants. Abraham is extremely important to both Jews and Christians as the one who first put his faith in God. Abraham's family grew larger and larger and began to fulfil the promise God made to Abraham **(look up**

Genesis chapter 12, verses 1 to 3). Most of the book of Genesis is about Abraham, his son, grandsons and great grandsons.

All of these sons became the leaders of large families called tribes. Later on the **tribe** of Levi was chosen by God to serve God in religious duties, especially in the

tabernacle, the special tent where God's people worshipped, and later on at the **temple** in Jerusalem. Moses and Aaron belonged to the tribe of Levi. Even up to Jesus' and Paul's day, Jewish people knew which tribe they belonged to. Jesus was from the tribe of Judah, and Paul belonged to Benjamin.

ABRAHAM AND SARAH

ISAAC AND REBEKAH

ESAU JACOB

LEAH'S SONS RACHEL'S SONS BILHAH'S SONS ZILPAH'S SONS

REUBEN JOSEPH DAN GAD
SIMEON BENJAMIN NAPHTALI ASHER
LEVI
JUDAH
ISSACHAR
ZEBULUN

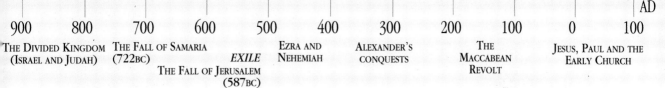

| 900 | 800 | 700 | 600 | 500 | 400 | 300 | 200 | 100 | 0 | AD 100 |

THE DIVIDED KINGDOM (ISRAEL AND JUDAH)

THE FALL OF SAMARIA (722BC)

THE FALL OF JERUSALEM (587BC)

EXILE

EZRA AND NEHEMIAH

ALEXANDER'S CONQUESTS

THE MACCABEAN REVOLT

JESUS, PAUL AND THE EARLY CHURCH

Genealogies

The history of a person's family is called a genealogy. Genealogies were very important to the Jews. They greatly respected elderly people and those who had lived before them, especially their parents and grandparents. Family honour and loyalty was very important and no-one would want to bring shame on their family. It was also very important in Abraham's family because God had chosen Isaac and his family in particular to receive his blessing.

There are many other genealogies in the Bible especially in the books of Numbers and 1 and 2 Chronicles. There are two genealogies of Jesus' family in the New Testament. Matthew chapter 1 gives us the family of Jesus' father, Joseph. Luke chapter 3 gives us the family of his mother, Mary. Most genealogies only included the men. However, you will find Rahab and Ruth in Matthew chapter 1, verse 5.

God and individuals

From the very beginning God has dealt with individual people like Abraham or Jacob. God was known as the God of Abraham, Isaac and Jacob. But he also deals with people as groups - families, tribes, nations, for example. People are held to be responsible for each other.

Names

The names given to people in Bible times were thought to be very important. Often they had a meaning. Abraham means "father of many nations". When Isaac was born, Sarah laughed out loud. Isaac means "someone laughs". Israel means "he wrestles with God". You will find more Bible names in the Who's Who? on pages 118-119.

Facts!

The Promised Land, also known as Canaan and Israel, lies between the Mediterranean Sea and the desert. It is part of a crescent-shaped area of fertile land which sweeps north through modern-day Iraq, then south towards Egypt. It has some very mountainous areas, especially in the south and some areas of desert. In Bible times it would also have been thickly wooded.

Did you know?

People seemed to live a very long time in Genesis. We are told that Adam died at 930 years old. The oldest man was Methuselah at 969. Abraham was 175 when he died. Isaac was 180 and Joseph was 110. How do we explain this? Some people believe that they counted the years differently in those days, but it is possible that people lived longer because life was healthier. Certainly, death only entered the world because of sin, and it may be that the overall effect of sin eventually shortened people's lifespan.

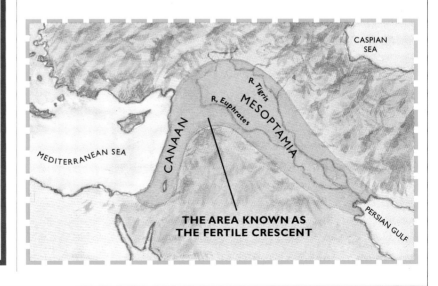

THE AREA KNOWN AS THE FERTILE CRESCENT

BC

| 2000 | 1900 | 1800 | 1700 | 1600 | 1500 | 1400 | 1300 | 1200 | 1100 | 1000 |

ABRAHAM, ISAAC, JACOB AND FAMILY

MOSES
AND THE
EXODUS

JOSHUA
AND
CONQUEST

DAVID
AND
SOLOMO

The long journey –
Exodus to Deuteronomy

Genesis and the books of Exodus to Deuteronomy make up the first five books of the Bible. They are called the Pentateuch (see page 16) or the Law of Moses. In many ways they are the most important part of the Old Testament. They are not just rules. There are a lot of stories too. The main story concerns how God took the people of Israel from slavery in Egypt to their own Promised Land in Canaan.

Israel become slaves

Genesis told us how Jacob's family went south into Egypt during a time of famine. You can read about that on page 28. Their descendants were there for about 400 years and became slaves of the Egyptians. The book of Exodus describes the rescue of the Israelites from slavery and how Moses led them out of Egypt and into the desert.

It was there that they received the Ten Commandments (see pages 36-37), but they were very disobedient, so it was forty years before God allowed them to reach the Promised Land. The Book of Joshua tells us how they entered and conquered it.

Wandering in the desert

The Book of Numbers continues the story of the journey from Egypt to the Promised Land. It describes how the **Israelites** lived in the desert and how they rebelled against God and against Moses. It also gives us long lists of the people who took part in that journey. God cared for each person. After the forty years in the desert, the Israelites reached the River Jordan and Moses looked across the river to Canaan, the land which God had promised to give them.

Moses' last sermon

Deuteronomy is like a long sermon from Moses before he dies. In Deuteronomy Moses reminds the Israelites of what had happened on their journey and points out to the people what God had done for them. Moses also tells them what God expects from them in the future. The Book of Leviticus contains in detail the laws which God expected his people to obey. It teaches them especially how they should worship God. It lists the duties of the priests and the sacrifices they had to offer.

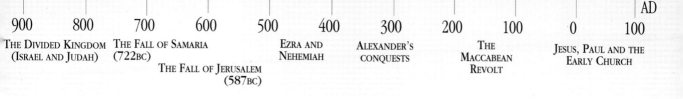

900	800	700	600	500	400	300	200	100	0	AD 100

THE DIVIDED KINGDOM
(ISRAEL AND JUDAH)

THE FALL OF SAMARIA
(722BC)

THE FALL OF JERUSALEM
(587BC)

EZRA AND
NEHEMIAH

ALEXANDER'S
CONQUESTS

THE
MACCABEAN
REVOLT

JESUS, PAUL AND THE
EARLY CHURCH

Did you know?

The names of the books in the Pentateuch (sounds like pen-tat-yook)

Genesis means beginning.

Exodus means the "way out" or departure.

Leviticus (le-vit-ee-kus) means Laws for the Levites who worked in the **tabernacle**.

Numbers gives lists of the people who left Egypt in the Exodus.

Deuteronomy (jute-er-on-omee) means the "second giving of the Law" by Moses.

God's great plan: the story so far

God created Adam and Eve to live in his perfect world, but they disobeyed him. People became so rebellious that God destroyed all except Noah and his family in the flood. Later, God chose Abraham to be the father of a new nation and promised the land of Canaan for them to live in. They became known as Israelites and they became slaves in Egypt. Moses led them out of Egypt and across the desert to the land of Canaan - the Promised Land.

EGYPTIAN SLAVES

The Egyptians needed slaves to build their great store-cities at Pithom and Rameses. They forced the Israelites to make mud bricks which were then dried in the sun. They refused to give them straw to strengthen the bricks **(look up Exodus chapter 5)**. They whipped them and didn't give them enough food. Sometimes they killed them.

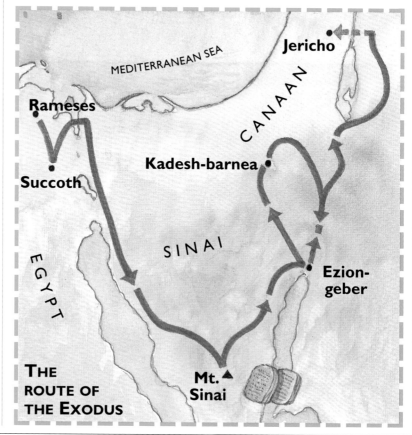

THE ROUTE OF THE EXODUS

MEDITERRANEAN SEA

Jericho

Rameses

CANAAN

Kadesh-barnea

Succoth

SINAI

Ezion-geber

EGYPT

Mt. Sinai

Moses the leader

Exodus 1-24

The young Moses

Moses was the son of Israelite slaves, but was brought up by an Egyptian princess - the daughter of Pharaoh. **You can find the story in Exodus chapter 2.** He had the very best education and grew up in the luxury of Pharaoh's palace. But the Egyptians were very cruel and Moses saw how badly the Israelites were treated. When he was about forty years old, Moses tried to help them. He murdered an Egyptian guard, and had to escape from Egypt. He then spent forty years as a shepherd in the desert of Sinai. God used this time to prepare him to be leader of the Israelites when they travelled across this same desert years later.

God calls Moses

One day, while Moses was looking after his flock near Mount Sinai, God spoke to him from a burning bush. God wanted Moses to rescue the Israelites. Moses was frightened and tried to get out of obeying God five times! **Look up Exodus chapters 3 and 4.** In the end Moses obeyed God and God gave him the courage to face up to Pharaoh. He also gave him power to perform miracles. This showed Pharaoh that God meant business. God also sent ten plagues to Egypt. After that Pharaoh agreed to let the Israelites leave Egypt.

Forty years in the desert

Moses was eighty when he led the Israelites out of Egypt. For the next forty years he taught the people and gave them God's Law. He also appointed leaders and judges for them. The Israelites had to fight many kings and tribes along the way, but Moses had more problems with the people themselves. Sometimes they were unfaithful and they kept grumbling. Even his sister Miriam and his brother Aaron turned against him. **You can read about this in Numbers, chapters 11 and 12.**

The attack

Moses sent Joshua, Caleb and ten other spies to report on how easy it would be to attack Canaan. All except Joshua and Caleb advised against it.

Moses led them eventually to the river Jordan, but God did not allow him to enter the Promised Land because he had earlier disobeyed God. **You can read about this in Numbers, chapter 20.** Joshua became the new leader of the Israelites. Moses died on top of a mountain from where he could see across the Promised Land. God buried him. **Look up Deuteronomy, chapter 34, verses 5 to 8.**

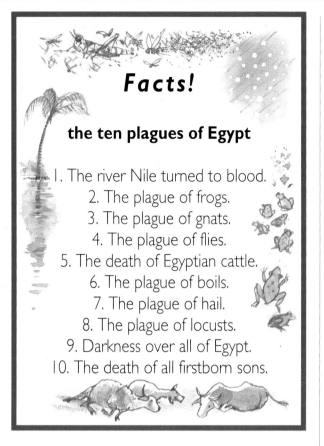

Facts!

the ten plagues of Egypt

1. The river Nile turned to blood.
2. The plague of frogs.
3. The plague of gnats.
4. The plague of flies.
5. The death of Egyptian cattle.
6. The plague of boils.
7. The plague of hail.
8. The plague of locusts.
9. Darkness over all of Egypt.
10. The death of all firstborn sons.

MIRACLES

God gave Moses the power to do three miracles in front of Pharaoh. First, Moses' stick turned into a snake. Then he made his hand become like a leper's, and finally changed water from the River Nile into blood. **You can read about this in Exodus chapter 4.** But Pharaoh's magicians were also able to copy by magic what Moses did.

WHY DID GOD SEND THE PLAGUES?

God sent ten plagues on the Egyptians to tell them to let his people go. **You can read about this in Exodus, chapters 7 to 11.** Many of these can be seen as natural disasters which often happened in Egypt. God's power is shown because he decided when and how they happened. The Egyptians suffered these things because Pharaoh was so stubborn and refused to let the Israelites leave Egypt.

PASSOVER

During the night, before the Israelites escaped from Egypt, the Israelites killed and roasted a lamb, which they ate standing up, ready to leave. They ate it quickly with bitter herbs and bread without yeast. They wiped some of the lambs' blood on their doorframes. When God sent his angel to kill all the firstborn sons of the Egyptians, the angel passed by the Israelites' houses with blood on the door posts. **You can read about it in Exodus chapter 12.** Even today, the Jewish feast of Passover still remembers this incident.

Did you know?

The word "paper" comes from papyrus, which is a sort of long grass which was made into baskets and even small boats. Moses was placed in a papyrus basket, then hidden amongst the high reeds which grew thickly in the shallow waters of the River Nile. The soft inside part of papyrus was beaten into flat sheets like paper. The Egyptians wrote and drew pictures on sheets of papyrus.

God's covenant with Israel

Exodus 19-24

What are covenants?

In those days, powerful nations sometimes made agreements, called treaties or covenants, with weaker nations whom they had defeated. Another example of a covenant is when two people get married and make serious promises to each other. At Mount Sinai, God made a covenant with the Israelites. He made promises to them but insisted that they should respond to him by obeying his Law.

The people meet God

Moses led the people through the desert to Mount Sinai where they would meet with God. There was thunder and lightning and a loud trumpet blast. Mount Sinai was covered with smoke. The people were very frightened and only Moses went up the mountain to speak with God. **You can read about this terrifying occasion in Exodus chapter 19.**

How God made the covenant

God began by laying out his commands especially in the Ten Commandments **(look up Exodus chapter 20, verses 1 to 17).** These were basic rules about how to treat God and each other, which God expected the Israelites to obey. Then, to confirm this agreement, God told Moses to take a bull and kill it. Moses took a bowl full of the bull's blood and sprinkled half of it over the people and poured out the other half in front of God's altar. This showed how serious this agreement was. It was a fresh start for God's people. **You can read about this in Exodus 24.**

Promises and curses

Israel had to obey God if they wanted to enjoy the wealth and peace that God had promised them. If they failed to be obedient, they would be punished. This might mean that he would stop blessing them or else he might send famine or disease or war. Sadly it did not take long for the people to have doubts and to find other gods (or **idols**) to worship. On one occasion they got Moses' brother, Aaron, to make a golden calf for them to worship. This was the first time that they seriously broke the covenant agreement with God. **You can read about it in Exodus 32.**

THE TEN COMMANDMENTS

1. **Worship no other god.**

2. **Do not worship idols.**

3. **Do not misuse God's name.**

4. **Keep God's special day holy.**

5. **Respect your parents.**

6. **Do not murder.**

7. **Do not take another man's wife.**

8. **Do not steal.**

9. **Do not accuse anyone falsely.**

10. **Do not desire other people's possessions.**

Did you know?

The idea of making covenants or treaties was common in Old Testament times. They might be matters of life and death, perhaps between two nations who might otherwise be at war. In the Bible, to show how serious an agreement or covenant is, people often killed an animal and shed its blood. When Jesus shed his blood on the cross, God was making a new covenant (see pages 84-85). From then on it was unnecessary to offer any more animal sacrifices.

Facts!

Mount Sinai was the place where God had spoken to Moses from the burning bush (see page 34). It was where God gave Moses the Ten Commandments. It is also called Mount Horeb in the Old Testament. At Sinai today there is the monastery of St Catherine where a very old manuscript of the Bible called Codex Sinaiticus was discovered in 1844.

A VERSE TO REMEMBER
"I am the Lord your God who brought you out of Egypt, where you were slaves. Worship no god but me."
(Exodus chapter 20, verses 2 and 3 GNB)

Journeys in the desert

Exodus 12-36, Numbers

From Goshen to the sea

The Exodus is the story of a great journey. The night before setting out, the people ate a meal with their families which is called the Passover (see page 35). From their place of slavery in Goshen, in Egypt, the Israelites travelled as far as the shallow water to the north of the Red Sea. When they got there, they discovered they were being pursued by Egyptian soldiers. They had no idea at all how they were going to cross the water. Suddenly God used a great wind to make a pathway through the water. When the Israelites were safe on the other side, the water flooded back to drown the Egyptian chariots, which were chasing after them. They were safe! They sang a song of praise to God and the women danced. They had escaped and had begun their long journey to the Promised Land.

Adventures in the desert

First they headed south to Mount Sinai, where Moses went up the mountain to meet with God. God gave him the Ten Commandments (see page 37) and other laws for the people to live by. Then they set out again, facing many dangers along the way. God guided them by a pillar of cloud by day and a pillar of fire at night. They experienced cold desert nights as well as the violent heat of the sun by day. They were always on the move and never knew how long the journey was going to last. There were always war-like desert tribes. **You can read about one battle, against their enemies Sihon and Og, in Numbers chapter 21, verses 21 to 35.** They were also always falling out, rebelling and complaining to Moses. Wild animals and snakes were also common in the desert.

A glimpse of the Promised Land

As they approached the Promised Land, God told them to send a group of twelve to spy out the land and to bring back some of its fruit. They brought back grapes, figs and pomegranates and reported that the land was rich. But all of them, except Joshua and Caleb, told stories of fearsome giants and fortified cities, and said how impossible it would be to conquer the land. God was very angry with them for not trusting him. He punished them and said that none of them would ever enter the Promised Land apart from Joshua and Caleb. **You can read this story in Numbers chapters 13 and 14.** It was Joshua who took over from Moses as leader and led them over the River Jordan into Canaan.

Did you know?

In the desert the Israelites remembered the meat, fish, cucumbers, water melons, leeks and onions which had been available in Egypt. Food in the desert must have been very poor. Water was hard to find. They complained bitterly. God sent small birds called quail for them to eat. He also sent manna which was like a wafer-biscuit and tasted of honey. Every day except for the Sabbath (Saturday), the Israelites gathered the manna for that day. God sent twice as much for them on the day before the Sabbath **(look up Exodus chapter 16)**. When the people first saw the manna lying in flakes on the ground they said "What is it?" – in their language "man hu". That is how manna got its name.

A TALKING DONKEY!

One of the strangest stories about the Israelites in the desert tells how an enemy called Balak tried to get a prophet called Balaam to help him defeat the Israelites. The story describes how Balaam's donkey actually spoke to advise him not to side with Balak. Instead, Balaam blessed the Israelites several times. **You can read this amazing story in Numbers chapters 22 to 24.**

The quail is a small game bird which migrates across the Sinai desert in huge flocks. The birds fly low and they were easily caught to provide food for the Israelites.

Facts!

The desert had a surprising amount of wildlife. There were small rodents like mice, but also wolves. Goats and sheep managed to live there, and some deer called gazelles could be found. There were a great many snakes and people were often bitten by them. **Look up Numbers chapter 21, verses 4 to 9 for a story about snakes.**

Laws and the tabernacle

Exodus 20-40, Leviticus

God had made a covenant with the Israelites (see pages 36-37). In return he wanted them to obey certain laws which covered all of their lives.

God's laws

God gave the Israelites laws about the **Sabbath** and other festivals. His laws also told them how to worship, how to settle arguments and what to do day by day. This included what they could wear, whom they could marry and what food they were allowed to eat. For example they were not to eat pork, rabbit or camel. **Look up Leviticus chapter 11.** It also covered what to do in times of illness, how to stay healthy and what to do if someone did wrong. God expected the people to be honest, respectful and kind, especially to women and children. God commanded them to offer food and shelter to strangers. He expected them to be loyal to him and not to go worshipping other gods. If the people were disobedient he would punish them.

Sacrifices

God told the Israelites how to worship him and what sacrifices to make. A **sacrifice** is something really special, like an animal or a bird or food, which is given to God. This was to thank God for something, to show God that they loved him or else to say sorry for some wrong which they had done. **You can read about the different sacrifices in Leviticus chapters 1 to 7.**

How to worship God

God told the Israelites to make a large tent called the **tabernacle**. This was to be used for worship and would be set up in the middle of the people's tents, wherever they stopped to camp. In the tabernacle, the priests made sacrifices on behalf of the people. Inside the tabernacle was a table on which fresh bread was laid and two altars. Altars are tables where sacrifices are placed. There was a lampstand with seven lamps, which were burnt all the time. There was also the **ark of the covenant**, a special wooden box covered with gold, containing the ten commandments. **Look up Exodus chapter 37, verses 1 to 9 to find out the size of the ark and what it looked like.**

Ark of the Covenant

incense altar

table for bread

basin

lampstand

altar for burnt offerings

FESTIVALS

The Israelites had three main festivals. Passover celebrated the Exodus when God saved Israel from Egypt. Pentecost is sometimes called the Feast of Weeks and celebrated the start of the grain harvest. The Feast of tabernacles was seven days long and was a kind of harvest festival. The people made small shelters to live in for a very brief time to remind them of how their ancestors wandered in the desert for forty years. These festivals sometimes had a great deal of feasting, music and dancing. Later in their history, the Israelites added other festivals.

Did you know?

One of God's laws said that people who owned vineyards were not to go back through their vineyard at harvest time to gather grapes they had missed or to pick up grapes that had fallen. These were to be left for poor people and foreigners. The corn growing at the edges of fields was also to be left uncut for them to gather.

PRIESTS

Aaron, Moses' brother, was the first High Priest. Priests led the people in worship at the tabernacle. Their main job was to prepare and offer the sacrifices which people brought to God. It was a very important thing to do for the people. The priests wore very colourful and special clothing **(look up Exodus chapter 28)**. The priests had helpers who were called Levites. Their jobs included looking after the tabernacle and its furnishings and carrying it when the people moved camp.

Facts!

God chose two men named Bezalel and Oholiab to be the craftsmen in charge of making the tabernacle and its furniture. They were skilled at designing and making things in gold, silver and wood. They used gifts of gold jewellery and cloth which the people brought to them to make beautiful things for the worship of God. Other people wove cloth in blue, purple and red and embroidered it with winged creatures. **Look up Exodus chapter 36, verses 8 to 38 to see how they made the tent.**

The conquest of Canaan

Joshua 1-11

Joshua becomes leader

God chose Joshua to help as Moses' assistant in the desert and then to take over from Moses as leader at the River Jordan before entering the Promised Land. He was more of an army commander than Moses and had already led the people in battle. **You can read about one occasion in Exodus chapter 17, verses 8 to 16.** To get into Canaan, the Israelites had to cross the River Jordan. God made the waters of the river pile up to the side just as he had done forty years before when they crossed the sea at the Exodus. Joshua led his soldiers through on dry land.

The battle of Jericho

The people of the land were called Canaanites, and God told Joshua to drive them out and destroy all of their religious places. This was because they were very sinful and God wanted the Israelites to be holy. Joshua sent spies to explore the city of Jericho in preparation for the attack. They were helped by a woman called Rahab who hid them in her house. **You can read the exciting story in Joshua chapter 2.** The spies brought back information and Joshua prepared to attack. In the first battle, Joshua led his men around the city of Jericho every day for six days. On the seventh day they marched around seven times, blew trumpets and shouted. The walls of the city fell down and Joshua and his soldiers captured it. **You can read the story in Joshua chapter 6.**

Conquering Canaan

The next city to be attacked was called Ai and this time Joshua sent only a small force. They were defeated because one man, Achan, had been disobedient. The next time Joshua attacked Ai, he destroyed the city. The Canaanites were now very worried and some of them from a place called Gibeon tricked Joshua. They pretended to have come a very long distance, and said they wanted to be Israel's servants. Joshua made peace with them, though he should not have done so, and the Gibeonites became their slaves. From then on Joshua gained more land, winning battles in the north and in the south. No-one was able to beat him, though many Canaanites were still left. When all the land had been taken, Joshua divided up the land equally amongst the twelve tribes of Israel.

Did you know?

After the battle of Jericho, Achan became greedy and wanted to keep some of what was captured for himself. God had ordered Israel to hand over any precious things that they captured. But Achan hid a beautiful cloak, some silver and a gold bar in his tent. After the Israelites had lost the battle of Ai, God showed Joshua what Achan had done. Achan was taken and stoned to death by the rest of the Israelites.

Facts!

Joshua varied his battle tactics. To capture Ai, Joshua sent thirty thousand of his best men to hide near the city. The next day, Joshua took the rest of his men and attacked the city. When the men of Ai came out for battle, the Israelites pretended they were afraid and ran away. Their enemies chased them, leaving the city with no one to defend it. Then Joshua held up his spear as a sign for the other soldiers to come out of hiding. They captured Ai and burnt it. They attacked and destroyed their enemies.

Twelve Israelite tribes entered Canaan with Joshua. They were the descendants of Jacob's twelve sons whom you can find on page 30. The Levites were not counted because they worked only in the **tabernacle.** So instead of them, Joseph's two sons, Ephraim and Manasseh, made up the twelve. The map shows how the land was eventually divided up between the tribes.

A VERSE TO REMEMBER
God said "Be strong and courageous. Do not be terrified; do not be discouraged, for the Lord your God will be with you wherever you go."
(Joshua chapter 1, verse 9 NIV)

The Judges
The Book of Judges

What was a judge?

"Judge" is the name given to a number of leaders or rulers of the Israelites up to the time of King Saul and King David. They were not "judges" as we know them today – people who sit in court and are responsible for the law. Basically they were leaders of one of the twelve tribes of Israel. Some of their stories are very famous, like Gideon and Samson. Some are not so well known. And they include women, like Deborah, who helped to win a battle. **Look up Judges chapters 4 and 5.**

A time when there was no king

The Book of Judges tells us what happened after Joshua and his army had taken over most of the Promised Land. The main problem was that the Israelites did not finish the job! They failed to obey God and drive out the Canaanites, who lived there, from the land. And after Joshua's death the Israelites began to forget God and all that he had done for them. They even began to worship the Canaanite gods, called the "Baals". The Book of Judges describes a time when there was much violence and evil in Israel. God allowed the Israelites to be defeated by other nations so that they began to beg him to help them. He would provide a judge to lead them, and, while the judge lived, the people obeyed God. But afterwards they returned to their old ways and forgot God again. **You can read about how this began in Judges chapter 2, verse 6 to chapter 3, verse 6.**

Famous judges

Another famous judge is Gideon, a member of the tribe of Manasseh. Like Moses before him, Gideon felt he was not strong enough to do what God commanded him. God reminded Gideon what God had done in the past and told him to rescue the Israelites from the Midianites. The Midianites used to come raiding on their camels and would steal animals and food from the Israelites. Gideon needed a lot of convincing, but in the end he led the Israelites to victory. **Look up his exciting story in Judges chapters 6 to 8.**

Samson was a great warrior from the tribe of Dan and is famous for his great strength and for his love for the Philistine woman Delilah. She tried very hard to ruin Samson and helped the Philistines to capture him. They cruelly blinded Samson but he finally destroyed them by causing the temple of their god Dagon to collapse on top of all who were gathered to worship Dagon and to celebrate Samson's defeat. **You can read Samson's story in Judges chapters 13 to 16.**

Gideon's army made a surprise attack on the Midianites at night and they fled in panic.

THE MIDIANITES

Unlike the Philistines, who were settlers, the Midianites were nomads in the desert (see pages 17 and 23), who traded with camels. Moses had married into the Midianite family of Jethro. They were the people who hired Balaam to curse Israel as they wandered through the desert (see page 39). Whenever the Midianites raided at harvest time, the Israelites would hide in caves in the hills.

Facts!

THE JUDGES OF ISRAEL

Othniel	who defeated the King of Aram
Ehud	the left-handed fighter
Shamgar	who killed 600 Philistines
Deborah	a mighty prophetess
Gideon	conqueror of the Midianites
Abimelech	who seized power for himself
Tola	leader for 23 years
Jair	leader for 22 years
Jephthah	who lost his daughter
Samson	who loved Delilah

Did you know?

Samson and John the Baptist were both Nazirites. They were men who were specially promised to be God's servants. They never cut their hair, never drank beer or wine, and never ate certain kinds of food. We are told that Samson's great strength came from the length of his hair, which was a sign of his dedication to God. The Nazirites are described in Numbers chapter 6.

CANAANITE GODS

Like the Egyptian gods, most of the gods of the Canaanites were nature gods. Baal and Asherah were expected to bring rain or to make the crops grow. When rain was scarce, the Israelites might be tempted to turn to these gods, so God commanded his people to destroy everything to do with them. The Philistines' chief god was called Dagon. Even in the time of Elijah, many years later, these gods were still a problem to Israel. **Look up 1 Kings 18 for the story of how Elijah faced the prophets of Baal.**

Baal, the most popular of the Canaanite gods.

A VERSE TO REMEMBER
"In those days Israel had no king; everyone did as he saw fit."
(Judges chapter 21, verse 25 NIV)

Ruth

The Book of Ruth

God at work in Moab!

Ruth lived during the time of the Judges in the neighbouring country of Moab. Moses was buried there and, at a much later time, King David sent his mother and father there to keep them safe. But the Moabites were often the enemies of the Israelites. They had tried to stop the Israelites crossing their land when they were on their way to Canaan and Solomon had Moabite wives who introduced false gods and evil practices. Israelites would not usually be friendly with a Moabitess like Ruth.

A story of two women

Ruth's mother-in-law, Naomi, was an Israelite woman. She had gone to live in Moab because of a famine in Israel. Her husband, Elimelech, and her sons, Mahlon and Chilion, had all died. Naomi had to look after herself and the wives of her two sons. One wife, Orpah, went home to her family, but Ruth stuck by Naomi. Naomi decided to go back home to Israel. Ruth said, "Wherever you go, I will go; wherever you live, I will live. Your people will be my people, and your God will be my God." Ruth showed that, even though she was not an Israelite, she could be part of God's great plan. She became an ancestor to both King David and Jesus.

A story of famine

Famine is common in the Bible. Some parts of Canaan were very fertile, but others needed a lot of hard work and rain at just the right time to produce crops. Abraham, Isaac, Jacob, David, Elijah, Elisha and Jeremiah all lived through times of famine. When the famine was over, Naomi and Ruth went back to Israel to work on the land of Naomi's relative, Boaz. Family responsibilities were taken very seriously and Boaz was expected to look after these two widows. He advised Ruth where it was best to work.

A story of rescue

Naomi wanted Boaz to save both herself and Ruth. So she advised Ruth to keep on working for Boaz. In the end, Boaz bought Naomi's field after meeting with the village elders and making sure that no-one had a better claim. Then he married Ruth to make sure that the land would remain in Naomi's family. They had a son called Obed whose grandson was King David.

Ruth and Naomi's journey from Moab to Israel was about 60 miles.

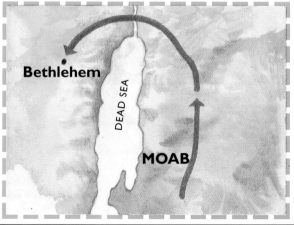

AGRICULTURE AND FARMING

Nomads travelled about to find food. Some tribes, like the Midianites, lived by raids to steal the crops and animals of others. But the Israelites were very settled and grew wheat, barley, lentils, peas and beans as well as vegetables like cucumbers and melons. One of the laws in the Book of Deuteronomy permitted poor people, like Ruth, to pick up the crops left by farmers at the end of harvest. **Look up Deuteronomy chapter 24, verse 19.**

FAMILY RESPONSIBILITY

Widows and orphans were amongst the weakest of people. They had no-one to look after them or to protect and provide for them. That is why Naomi went back to Israel, so that she might find one of her family to look after her. Boaz was a close relative and saw it as his responsibility to look after Naomi and Ruth. Naomi wanted to sell her husband's field, so Boaz made sure that anyone who bought the field should also look after Ruth. In the end Boaz himself bought the field and married Ruth. **You can read about how people bought and sold land in Leviticus chapter 25, verses 23 to 25.**

Samuel and Saul

1 Samuel 1-31

A time of change

We have seen that during the time of the judges everyone did just as they pleased. Samuel was the last of the judges and prepared the way for Israel to have kings. Samuel's parents, Elkanah and Hannah, had waited a long time for a son. They were so grateful to God for Samuel that they promised to give him to God. So Samuel became servant of the priest, Eli, whose own sons were evil even though they were priests. God spoke to Samuel in the middle of the night and told him that he would punish both Eli and his sons. **You can read this story in 1 Samuel chapter 3.**

Capturing the ark

Early on in Samuel's time as a judge, the Philistines attacked the Israelites and captured the **ark of the covenant.** They put it in the temple of their god, Dagon, but Dagon kept falling over in front of it. Everything went wrong for the Philistines. In the end, their priests advised them to return the ark to the Israelites.

Samuel the king-maker

The Israelites began to beg Samuel for a king to lead them in battle like other nations. Samuel was very sad about this because it seemed that they were losing their trust in God. But God pointed out the right man. At first Saul was not keen to become king and he hid when Samuel sent for him. But Saul was very tall and handsome and a good fighter. The people thought he would make a good king. **Look up the story in 1 Samuel chapter 10.** At first Saul trusted God and defeated the Ammonites, the Philistines and the Amalekites in battle, helped by his son, Jonathan.

King Saul's rival

Sadly Saul did not remain obedient to God. God told Samuel that he had rejected Saul as king. He showed Samuel that a young shepherd boy named David was to be the next king. David quickly became famous after he had killed the Philistine giant Goliath. Saul became jealous of him and tried to kill David many times. After many years of chasing David in the desert, Saul was finally killed in battle with the Philistines.

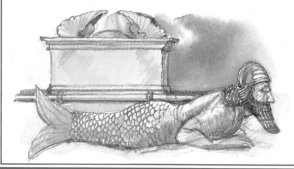

Did you know?

When kings or priests were appointed in those days, it was common for an important person, like a priest, to pour oil over their heads as a sign that they had been chosen and prepared by God. It was a sign that God had poured out his spirit upon them.

You can read about how David was chosen and anointed in 1 Samuel 16, verses 1 to 13.

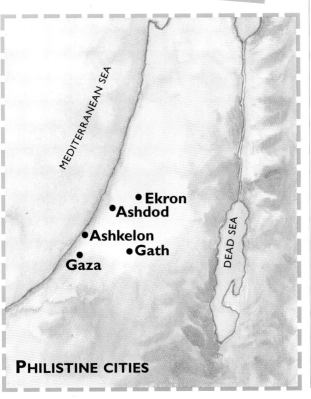

PHILISTINE CITIES

MEDITERRANEAN SEA

• Ekron
•Ashdod
•Ashkelon
•Gath
•
Gaza

DEAD SEA

SAUL'S FAMILY

Jonathan is Saul's most famous son. He was a great warrior and became a firm friend of David, even helping David to escape from his father. Their friendship is described in 1 Samuel 20. David also married one of Saul's daughters, Michal, who later disliked David.

Facts!

This was the Iron Age and both the Israelite army and its opponents used iron weapons, including swords, daggers, spears and shields. Strangely there were no blacksmiths in Israel and the Israelites even had to go to the Philistines to get their weapons sharpened. Although King Saul organised a regular army, we would find their battles very disorganised with people running around all over the place. It was basically quite a small army, made up of ordinary people. When bigger nations like the Egyptians or, later on, the Assyrians and Babylonians attacked, the Israelites did not really stand a chance.

A VERSE TO REMEMBER
" The Lord then stood beside Samuel and called out as he had done before, 'Samuel! Samuel!' 'I'm listening,' Samuel answered. 'What do you want me to do?'"
(1 Samuel chapter 3, verse 10 CEV)

David the shepherd boy

1 Samuel 16-31

The youngest son of Jesse

Saul, Israel's first king, had failed because he stopped trusting in God. Some time before Saul died, God had sent Samuel to the family of Jesse to choose a new king. To Samuel's surprise it was David, Jesse's youngest son, who was to be God's chosen king. His seven elder brothers were amazed! But God saw that David loved him. **This story is told in 1 Samuel, chapter 16.**

A shepherd boy

Looking after the sheep was the job of the youngest son. What David learnt as a shepherd helped him throughout his life. It taught him how to look after and lead others. David became a great leader of men. It also taught him how to look after himself in the wild. This was very important for him because King Saul very quickly became jealous of David and chased him around the desert of Judah for many years before David became king. Finally, his experience as a shepherd taught him about God. **You can read about this in Psalm 23 where David describes God as his own shepherd.** God provided for David and looked after him and protected him.

A great fighter

David proved himself as a fighter. His first famous battle was with the Philistine giant Goliath. The rest of the Israelite army, including David's brothers, were too terrified to fight, but David put all of his trust in God. **Read how he did this in 1 Samuel chapter 17.** King Saul became jealous and David had to escape from him. He led a band of men in the desert. He was often chased by Saul and twice refused to take the king's life even though Saul was trying to kill him. He also fought against the Philistines and rescued the town of Keilah from them. All through this time, Jonathan, one of Saul's sons, remained David's friend. Jonathan must have found it very difficult to be the friend of his father's enemy.

A poet

King Saul and his three sons, Jonathan, Abinadab and Malchishua, were all killed in their final battle against the Philistines. David wrote a poem in memory of them - "It was easy to love Saul and Jonathan. Together in life, together in death; they were faster than eagles and stronger than lions." His poem is called a lament. **You can read it in 2 Samuel chapter 1, verses 19 to 27.**

THE BOOK OF PSALMS

Seventy-three of the psalms are recorded as David's. This great collection, the biggest book of the Bible, contains many songs of praise, prayers for vengeance, celebrations of God's faithfulness or his goodness. Many other subjects are covered. Psalm 119 is the longest with 176 verses, but some are quite short. The most famous one is probably Psalm 23, which begins "The Lord is my shepherd".

SHEPHERDS

Being a shepherd was a dangerous and lonely job, working in the fields for long hours. The shepherd led his sheep from one bit of grazing to the next, fighting off lions, bears and wolves which attacked the sheep. They were not thought of as important people and had a bad reputation for theft and violence. But shepherds did a useful job and the Bible often describes God as a shepherd, who faithfully looks after his people in spite of all difficulties.

MUSIC

David was a singer, harpist and composer of psalms. He first went to King Saul's court as a musician to entertain the king. We know very little about the music of those days. It was probably quite simple. **In 1 Chronicles chapter 25 you can read about the musicians whom David organised to lead the worship of God in the Temple**.

Did you know?

The Philistines were the main enemies of the Israelites right up to the time of King David, who finally destroyed them. They had settled on the south-western coast of Canaan before the Israelites arrived. They were very fierce fighters with better weapons than the Israelites. Their name gives us the word "Palestine".

A VERSE TO REMEMBER
"People judge others by what they look like, but I judge people by what is in their hearts."
(1 Samuel chapter 16, verse 7 CEV)

David the king
2 Samuel

King in the making

David, the shepherd boy, became leader of a band of outlaws. They were disappointed in King Saul's rule. Some may have been robbers and murderers. David and this band were always on the run from Saul. Following Saul's death, David was crowned king in Hebron, a city in Judah. David was a member of the southern tribe of Judah and it was the obvious place for him to choose as his base. He was thirty years of age. The way was soon paved for David to be king over the whole country. His rival, Ishbosheth, was Saul's only surviving son. But when he and Abner, the commander of his army, were murdered, no-one could offer a challenge to David any more. He moved his capital to Jerusalem, which is often called the City of David.

A popular king

David fought many wars and overcame all of the nations round about. He defeated the Philistines, the Ammonites and the Syrians. He also took the **ark of the covenant**, the symbol of God's presence with the Israelites, to Jerusalem. He built himself a palace and wanted to build a temple there, but God did not allow him to because he had killed so many people in battle. God promised that David's son would build one. So David collected materials to be used in building the temple. **Look up 1 Chronicles chapter 22, verses 2 to 5 to see what David collected.**

THE ARK OF THE COVENANT - BRINGING IT UP TO JERUSALEM

For hundreds of years since their wanderings in the desert, the ark of the covenant had been the symbol of God's presence with the Israelites. David wanted it to be in his new capital city of Jerusalem. It was carried in procession into the city. David and his people celebrated by dancing along the way. When it was safely in its place, David offered sacrifices to God and gave gifts of food to the people.

Things get worse

David also made mistakes and did many wrong things. One day he saw Bathsheba, the wife of Uriah, one of David's soldiers. David wanted to sleep with her. So he arranged for Uriah to be killed in the front line of the battle and then took Bathsheba to be his own wife. In those days it was quite common for wealthy men to have more than one wife. This practice is called polygamy (see page 27). The prophet Nathan accused him of wrong and David admitted his sin. His words of sorrow are recorded in Psalm 51.

The time of rebellions

David had set a bad example and his son Absalom plotted a rebellion against his father. **You can read the story of Absalom's rebellion in 2 Samuel, chapters 13 to 18**. Another rebellion began under Sheba, but once again Joab, the commander of David's army, put it down. David's reign ended sadly with more bloodshed. He became very weak, but in his love for God he had been a "man after God's own heart". He is remembered as Israel's greatest king.

JOAB

In many ways Joab was David's right-hand man. He helped to secure the throne for David and frequently led the army for him. He was a great fighter, but was ruthless and bloodthirsty. He killed Abner to help make David king of all Israel. He also killed Absalom in the rebellion against his father David. As Jesus said, "all who take the sword will die by the sword". **Look up Matthew chapter 26, verse 52**.

FAMILY TROUBLES

David's son, Absalom, wanted to take over as king. So he tried to win the people over to himself. He half succeeded and many followed him so that David had to escape from Jerusalem to avoid being killed. Absalom was killed by Joab, the commander of David's army, when he got caught in a tree by his hair. David was overcome with grief. David had several other sons and there was confusion about who would be the next king. In the end David ordered that Solomon, the son of David and Bathsheba, should be anointed king.

Did you know?

It was David who first made Jerusalem the capital. **Read how he captured it by surprise attack in 2 Samuel chapter 5, verses 6 to 10**. It is sometimes known as the "city of David". It was an easy place to defend because it was high up on a hill. Solomon built his temple there, so from then on it was where the king lived and where the main worship of God took place.

King Solomon

1 Kings 1-11

Brothers and half-brothers

Solomon's mother was Bathsheba. But David had several wives and some of them had sons who were half-brothers to Solomon. So he was not the only one who might have expected to become king after David. This was bound to cause problems. Solomon's reign began with much bloodshed as he destroyed rivals such as Adonijah and Shimei. He also sent the priest Abiathar far away and had Joab, his father David's great warrior, killed.

Solomon's wisdom

The Israelites always looked back to Solomon's reign as a time when they had been very wealthy and respected. Solomon was thought to have been an incredibly wise king and encouraged schools of wisdom. The books of wisdom in the Bible, like Proverbs, Ecclesiastes, Job and the Song of Songs, look back to Solomon as their source. **You can read about how Solomon prayed for wisdom in 1 Kings chapter 3**. This chapter describes how Solomon decided what was just in a very difficult case.

Did you know?

Proverbs are wise sayings which sum up the truth about a particular subject. The book of Proverbs in the Bible has many wise sayings about work, justice, family life and relationships, how to behave in different situations and a lot of other practical matters.

VERSES TO REMEMBER

- some proverbs

"Respect and obey the Lord!
This is the beginning of wisdom."
(Proverbs chapter 9, verse 10 CEV)

"The Lord hates anyone who cheats,
but he likes everyone who is honest."
(Proverbs chapter 11, verse 1 CEV)

"Kind words are good medicine,
but deceitful words can really hurt."
(Proverbs chapter 15, verse 4 CEV)

Solomon's wealth

A wise person was expected to be rich and Solomon was certainly very rich. He built a luxurious palace for himself and a great temple for the worship of God. Foreign kings, like Hiram king of Tyre, had been friends with David, and they continued their friendship with Solomon. So he enjoyed peace as well as the gifts such as cedarwood which Hiram sent to him to help build the temple. Amongst other things, he possessed over 500 golden shields. He had a large throne of gold and ivory and used golden cups and plates. Silver was cheap for Solomon. He had a huge fleet of ships, 1,400 chariots and 12,000 horses. The Queen of Sheba came from Arabia to visit Solomon because she had heard about his wisdom and all he had done. **You can read about this in 1 Kings chapter 10.** She was very impressed. But being wealthy often causes problems. Solomon turned away from God and began to worship the false gods which his many wives worshipped. At the end of his forty year reign, he had many enemies and God told him that his kingdom would break up and be divided.

SOLOMON'S TEMPLE

This was a great building of three floors high and it took 30,000 men seven years to build it out of great blocks of stone and beautiful wood with gold and silver. None of the noisy work was done nearby because the **temple** was meant to be a holy place. Right at the centre of the temple was the **most holy place,** where God's presence was to be sought. The covenant box was placed there.

FOREIGN GODS

Solomon had many wives. Some of them were not Israelites and worshipped other gods. In later years their influence became a great problem for the Israelites. Solomon had Moabite wives who encouraged him in the dreadful worship of Chemosh, which sometimes encouraged the sacrifice of children. He also began to worship other gods and was not true to the God of Israel.

Facts!

Solomon traded with Hiram of Tyre and received gold as well as cedarwood from Lebanon. He also had his sailors go to a land called Ophir. They returned with 14,000 kilogrammes of gold. When the Queen of Sheba visited him, Solomon was able to shower her with gifts. She brought him gifts of gold, jewels and spices.

Israel – the northern kingdom

1 and 2 Kings, Hosea, Amos, Jonah, Nahum

A kingdom divided

King Solomon tried to kill all his enemies and control the Israelites by force, but this failed. After his death, two men struggled to become leader. Solomon's son, Rehoboam (Ray-ha-boam), was one of them. The other was Jeroboam, who had been in charge of Solomon's slaves. The northern tribes supported Jeroboam. This struggle led to the division of Solomon's kingdom into two parts. The northern kingdom was called Israel and the southern kingdom was called Judah. This was how the country remained for about 200 years until the Assyrians (Ass-iri-ans) destroyed the northern capital, Samaria, in 722 BC.

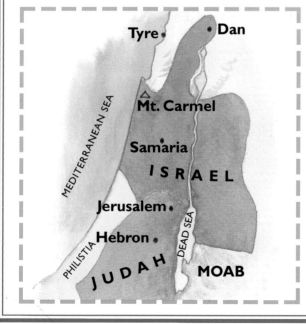

The northern kingdom

For the next two hundred years, all the kings of the northern kingdom were like Jeroboam in two ways. Firstly, he grabbed the crown for himself by violence. Secondly, he turned away from God and began to worship other gods. One of the worst of these northern kings is King Ahab and his Canaanite wife, Jezebel. **You can read their story in 1 Kings, chapters 18 to 22.**

Two prophets

Prophets are God's messengers. Amos and Hosea were prophets whom God sent to Israel during this time. God called Amos from his work as a farm-hand to take God's message to the northern kingdom. He told them that God the Creator loved them and cared for them. But God is also holy and cares for justice. So Amos pointed out how badly the Israelites treated the poor and weak. **Look at Amos chapter 2, verses 6 to 8.**

Hosea's life was very like his message. God wanted him to tell the Israelites how they had been unfaithful to him by worshipping **idols.** So God told Hosea to marry an unfaithful woman, named Gomer. She had relationships with other men as well as being the wife of Hosea. Hosea now knew from experience what it was like to suffer what God suffered because the Israelites had stopped loving him. He was also able to say how much

God loved them and would never stop loving them.

The end of the northern kingdom

Throughout this period Israel and Judah were almost always at war with each other. Israel was also attacked twice by the Syrians from the north. But the end of the kingdom of Israel came when the terrifying Assyrians attacked and destroyed Samaria in 722 BC. The Israelites were taken into exile in Assyria. Many never came back to their homeland.

Jonah

The prophet Jonah is famous for running away from God's call and being swallowed up by a great fish. But the reason why he ran away is that God told him to preach to the Assyrians in Nineveh. He may have been frightened, but he certainly must have found it difficult to imagine that God could want to offer forgiveness to such people! **Try reading what else happened in the Book of Jonah**.

Nahum

The Israelite prophet Nahum lived in the southern kingdom of Judah, just before the time when Assyria was destroyed. In his exciting prophecy, the Book of Nahum in the Old Testament, he predicts the fall of Nineveh with flashing chariots dashing through the streets, attackers rushing to the walls, dead bodies everywhere and terror and confusion all around. **You can read Nahum's description in Nahum chapter 2**.

Facts!

The Assyrians were very brutal warriors and their cruelty was greatly feared. They were effective fighters and made good use of chariots. They used siege ramps and battering rams to attack walled cities. When they conquered a country, they would take great numbers of people from their homes and make them live somewhere else, in exile. Nobody was sad when they were conquered and their capital, Nineveh, destroyed in 612 BC.

A VERSE TO REMEMBER
"The Lord is powerful yet patient; he makes sure
that the guilty are always punished."
(Nahum chapter 1, verse 3 CEV)

Elijah and Elisha

1 Kings 17-21; 2 Kings 1-8, 13

Both Elijah and Elisha lived in the northern kingdom of Israel. They are the first important prophets which we read about in the Bible, though Moses is sometimes described as a prophet. In the Bible, a prophet is someone to whom God gives a message to pass on.

Prophets and kings

Elijah and Elisha appeared at a time when things were going badly wrong in Israel. King Ahab and his Canaanite wife, Jezebel, had encouraged the worship of Baal (see page 45). The Bible tells us nothing about Elijah's early life. He was a man of the desert who told King Ahab that he should worship God. Elijah predicted that there would be no rain. After three years he challenged the prophets of Baal to a contest on Mount Carmel to see whose god could set fire to a sacrifice which was soaked with water. **You can read about**

this dramatic encounter in 1 Kings chapter 18. The people were convinced of God's power but King Ahab did not change his ways.

Elisha was a prophet during the time when the Syrians, from the country to the north-east of Israel, laid siege to the capital Samaria. Then God did an extraordinary thing. He made the Syrian army hear the sound of a great army arriving. They panicked and ran away, leaving their camp completely empty! **Look up 2 Kings, chapters 6 and 7, for the story**.

An age of injustice

There was much injustice in Israel at the time. On one occasion, King Ahab and his wife Jezebel murdered a good man called Naboth so that they could steal his vineyard. Elijah bravely went to tell King Ahab that God would judge him, that dogs would lick up Jezebel's blood and that the rest of his family would be destroyed one day.

Men of power

Both Elijah and Elisha did many miracles. Once, Elijah was staying at the house of a poor widow. God provided food for her by making sure that her flour and oil did not run out so that she could make bread. On another famous occasion, Naaman, the commander of the Syrian army, who was suffering from leprosy, came to Elisha. The prophet told him to wash seven times in the River Jordan. When Naaman did this he was cured. **You can read the story of Naaman in 2 Kings, chapter 5.**

When Elijah came to the end of his life God took him up to heaven in a chariot of fire, leaving Elisha to carry on his work. Although Elijah's followers looked for his body, they never found it.

Facts!

Naaman, commander of the Syrian army, had leprosy. The word "leprosy" is used in the Bible to cover a number of skin diseases. This was greatly feared in Bible times and still exists today in some countries. It makes the skin discoloured and the fingers and toes of the sufferer begin to fall off. Sufferers usually lived in places called "colonies" far away from other people.

Did you know?

Bread was a basic food for everyone right through Bible times. In Elijah's time, people made flour at home by grinding wheat or barley between two stones. The flour was mixed with olive oil and some yeast to make a dough. The dough was shaped into small round loaves and baked in an oven made of pottery with a fire underneath.

ELIJAH AND JOHN THE BAPTIST

The Israelites began to believe that Elijah would return because his dead body was never found. They believed he would announce the arrival of the Messiah. The prophet Malachi, in chapter 4, verse 5, writes, "But before the great and terrible day of the Lord comes, I will send you the prophet Elijah"(GNB). The writers of the gospels in the New Testament say that John the Baptist was the person Malachi meant. **Read about him in Matthew chapter 3, verses 1-12.**

Judah – the southern kingdom

1 and 2 Kings, Micah, Zephaniah, Jeremiah

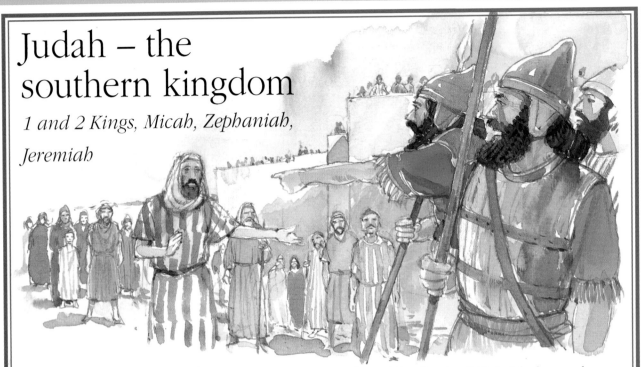

King Hezekiah

The northern kingdom had Samaria as its capital, but Judah's capital city remained Jerusalem with its temple. The southern kingdom of Judah tended to have better kings. Kings like Asa, Hezekiah (Hez-e-kya) and Josiah (Jos-eye-a) tried their best to make sure that Judah worshipped the one true God. Hezekiah faced the same threat from the Assyrians as the northern kingdom of Israel. The Assyrian army commander gave Hezekiah a threatening message from his king, Sennacherib. He boasted that he would attack and capture Jerusalem. But Hezekiah was encouraged by the prophet Isaiah (Eye-sye-a) who said that God would protect the city. Hezekiah stood firm. **You can read about this in 2 Kings chapters 18 to 20**.

King Josiah

King Josiah is famous because he encouraged the people to obey God's law and he did away with pagan worship. **His story is written in 2 Kings chapters 22 and 23**. The Book of Habakkuk may have been written just after Josiah's reforms and seems to say that very little changed. Habakkuk keeps asking why God lets it all happen, but is determined to keep on trusting God in spite of everything.

More prophets

The southern kingdom also had many more prophets than the northern kingdom to bring God's word to the people. Micah was one of the first and the Book of Micah is a collection of his prophecies. He told the people of Judah that God is holy, loving and just. Micah chapter 6, verse 8, sums up Micah's message: "The Lord God has told us what is right and what he demands: 'See that justice is done, let mercy be your first concern, and humbly obey your God.'" (CEV) Another two prophets, Zephaniah and Jeremiah, have fairly gloomy messages. They warned the people that God was going to judge the kingdom of Judah and that they could not escape punishment.

Defeat and exile

Sadly, it was not long before Judah was also attacked and defeated. This was in 597 BC and this time the invasion came from the Babylonians. They had taken over from the Assyrians as the main power in the area. Jerusalem, including Solomon's Temple, was completely destroyed in 587 BC and many of the people were carried off into **exile** in Babylon.

EVEN GOOD KINGS...

In 1 Kings chapter 15, verse 14 we read, "As long as Asa lived, he was completely faithful to the Lord, even though he did not destroy the local shrines." (CEV) Even the good kings, like King Asa, failed to obey God in everything and allowed the people to go on worshipping other gods.

ARMY WIPED OUT

When the Assyrian king Sennacherib (Sen-ak-er-ib) threatened Jerusalem his army was destroyed by an angel of God, just as Isaiah had foretold. One hundred and eighty-five thousand dead soldiers filled his camp. Sennacherib went back to his capital, Nineveh, where he was murdered by his sons whilst he was worshipping his god. **Read about how this happened in 2 Kings chapter 19, verses 35 to 37.**

Did you know?

While Hezekiah was king, the prophet Isaiah told him that he was going to die. Hezekiah was very troubled. He prayed to God to spare him and Isaiah brought the message that God had agreed to allow him fifteen more years to live. Hezekiah asked for a sign to prove that this would happen. God made the shadow cast by the sun on a stairway go back ten steps. Archaeologists suggest that this was a stairway specially built to tell the time. **You can read about this in 2 Kings chapter 20, verses 1 to 11.**

A VERSE TO REMEMBER

"Fig trees may no longer bloom, or vineyards produce grapes; olive trees may be fruitless, and harvest time a failure; sheep-pens may be empty, and cattle stalls vacant - but I will still celebrate because the Lord God saves me." (Habakkuk chapter 3, verses 17 to 18 CEV)

Isaiah the prophet
The Book of Isaiah

One of the most important prophets in the Bible is Isaiah. The Book of Isaiah has 66 chapters and contains some of the most famous passages in the Old Testament. New Testament writers quote from Isaiah more frequently than from almost any other book of the Old Testament.

Who was Isaiah?

Isaiah seems to have come from a wealthy and important family. He lived in Jerusalem and possibly served King Uzziah as a writer and historian. He was also a poet, as well as being a prophet and teacher. The messages recorded in his book contain psalms in praise of God, direct messages to the people of God and Isaiah's thoughts about events which were happening at the time. He could see that God was going to send the Israelites into **exile** in Babylon. He tried to prepare them for it with messages explaining what God was doing.

Isaiah's call

Isaiah chapter 6 records the prophet's call to be God's special messenger. He was worshipping in the temple when suddenly he saw the glory of God himself. God was seated on a heavenly throne surrounded by strange heavenly creatures called cherubim and seraphim. God's kingly cloak was so great that it filled the whole temple. The heavenly creatures were worshipping God, the temple shook and

Isaiah was very frightened. But God called him to take his message to the people even though they might not be willing to hear it.

Isaiah's message

Like many others of God's messengers, Isaiah was very angry at the injustice he found in Israelite society. For Isaiah this was an insult to a holy God. But in a famous passage he predicts that "a young woman who is pregnant will have a son and will name him Immanuel" (Isaiah chapter 7, verse 14 GNB). Christians believe that this prophecy was fulfilled when Jesus was born. Later on the prophet promises:

"A child has been born for us. We have been given a son who will be our ruler. His names will be Wonderful Advisor and Mighty God, Eternal Father and Prince of Peace." (Isaiah chapter 9, verse 6 CEV).

Some of the most famous parts of Isaiah can be found in chapters 40 to 55. These chapters are mostly encouragement to the Israelites in exile. Isaiah explains that God has not forgotten them. Isaiah uses picture language to show what God is like. He says that the name Jerusalem is carved on God's hands. He also says that God carries them like a shepherd carrying a lamb. Isaiah reminds them that their God is far more powerful than the idols which the Babylonians worship and which must be carried around by men. In his own good time, God will take them back to Jerusalem.

THE SERVANT OF THE LORD

Chapters 40 to 55 of Isaiah introduce a character called the Servant of the Lord. Jews see this figure as a picture of the Israelites at their most faithful. But Christians see the Servant as a prophecy of the Lord Jesus Christ. Chapter 53 describes how the Servant will be rejected by people and badly treated. The Servant will be condemned to death and killed because of the evil things which people have done. Verse 12 says "...he suffered for our sins and asked God to forgive us."

A VERSE TO REMEMBER
"He was wounded and crushed because of our sins; by taking our punishment, he made us completely well."
(Isaiah chapter 53, verse 5 CEV)

Did you know?

The Bible sometimes describes Israel as a vineyard. Isaiah wrote a song describing a man who planted a vineyard. He worked hard, digging and clearing away the stones. He planted vines and built a watchtower to keep guard. He dug a pit for treading the grapes when they were ripe. But when the grapes were ready, they turned out to be sour. Isaiah said that the people were like vines planted by God. God had expected them to be good but instead they did evil things. **You can find Isaiah's song in Isaiah chapter 5, verses 1 to 7.**

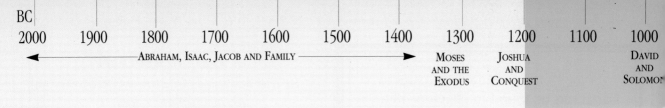

BC										
2000	1900	1800	1700	1600	1500	1400	1300	1200	1100	1000

◄——— ABRAHAM, ISAAC, JACOB AND FAMILY ———►

MOSES AND THE EXODUS

JOSHUA AND CONQUEST

DAVID AND SOLOMON

Israel: God's chosen people

Joshua, Judges, 1 and 2 Samuel, 1 and 2 Kings, 1 and 2 Chronicles

At this point we pause in the story about God's great plan for his people to look back at what has happened. These books of the Bible tell us the story of the Israelites from the time they entered the Promised Land to the time when God sent them into exile. This covers a period of more than six hundred years.

Back to the beginning
The Israelites always traced themselves back to Abraham, Isaac and Jacob. Jacob's name had been changed to Israel by God and he had twelve

sons. Their descendants were the twelve tribes of Israel. But it was the Exodus which really made the Israelites into a nation. For the first time, under Moses as leader, they began to be responsible together for how they lived and settled their quarrels. They now had laws and

particular ways of doing things like worshipping God and going to war.

Settling down
It was under their leader, Joshua, that they finally settled down in the Promised Land. They became more and more like one nation and, although the twelve tribes still existed, in the end they accepted one leader, a king. The first kings were Saul, David and Solomon. Slowly the kings who succeeded them became more and more like the kings of other nations. Israelite kings fought other kings and became great. They also began to lead the Israelites into worshipping other gods and doing the evil things which other nations did. They turned away from God.

Dividing into two kingdoms
Sadly, the Israelites began to divide into two kingdoms - the northern state of Israel and the southern state of Judah. In their turn, these states were eventually crushed by invaders. The Assyrians, who were their northern neighbours, defeated Israel and destroyed Samaria, the capital of the Israelites. Then they carried the people off into exile. They never returned. The prophet Jeremiah had warned that this would happen to Judah as well. More than a hundred years later, the Babylonians attacked Judah and its capital, Jerusalem. They carried the people of Judah off into exile. Seventy years later, they began to return to Judah and Jerusalem.

900	800	700	600	500	400	300	200	100	0	100 AD

THE DIVIDED KINGDOM (ISRAEL AND JUDAH)   THE FALL OF SAMARIA (722BC)   *EXILE*   EZRA AND NEHEMIAH   ALEXANDER'S CONQUESTS   THE MACCABEAN REVOLT   JESUS, PAUL AND THE EARLY CHURCH

THE FALL OF JERUSALEM (587BC)

The exiles from Judah entered Babylon through the splendid Ishtar Gate

A people in exile

Once again, the Israelites were living in someone else's country as they had done hundreds of years earlier in Egypt. Once again they were not in control of their own future. The chosen people had to come to terms with the fact that God had allowed them to lose most of what he had promised them. This was a very hard lesson to learn. But God had made it very clear right at the beginning that disobedience would lead to them being punished. Joshua had made this clear when he gathered the people together to make promises to God –

"He is a holy God and will not forgive your sins. He will tolerate no rivals, and if you leave him to serve foreign gods, he will turn against you and punish you. He will destroy you, even though he was good to you before." (Joshua chapter 24, verses 19 and 20 GNB)

WHY DID GOD CHOOSE THE ISRAELITES?

"You were the weakest of all nations, but the Lord chose you because he loves you and because he had made a promise to your ancestors." (Deuteronomy chapter 7, verses 7 and 8 CEV)

A VERSE TO REMEMBER

"God says 'But I know your deeds and your thoughts, and I will make sure you get what you deserve.'" (Jeremiah chapter 17, verse 10 CEV)

Did you know?

Who was the weeping prophet? Jeremiah was called to be a prophet even before he was born. He began to speak God's message in Jerusalem during the reign of King Josiah and continued until the people of Judah were carried off into exile. He is sometimes known as the "weeping prophet" because his message is very sad. God told him that he was about to punish Judah. Jeremiah described Judah as a clay pot which God would have to break and remake. **You can read his words in Jeremiah chapter 18, verses 1 to 17**. Although he was a very good man, Jeremiah did not escape punishment. He was treated very badly by his people and, like them, was carried off into exile, probably into Egypt.

Defeat and exile

2 Kings 25, Ezekiel

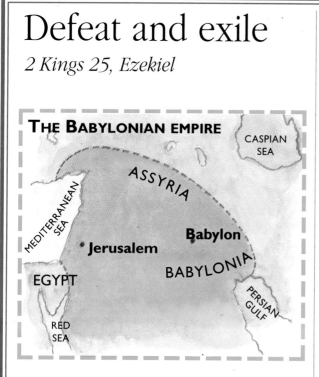

The Fall of Jerusalem and the temple

Zedekiah (Zed-e-ky-a) was the last king of Judah. The country was by now part of the Babylonian empire which reached as far west as Egypt. Zedekiah rebelled against Babylon. Nebuchadnezzar, King of Babylon, came and attacked him and killed his two sons in front of him. Then he blinded Zedekiah, put him in chains and dragged him off to Babylon. In 587BC, Jerusalem with all its important buildings, including the temple, was burnt down.

It was very difficult for the Israelites to understand how the temple could be destroyed, because they believed that it was the place where God was present in a special way. Their confusion is well expressed in the Book of Lamentations. **Look up Lamentations chapter 1, verses 1 to 11 to see how they felt**. They had to learn that God was present everywhere, even in Babylon, and not just in the temple.

Living in exile

The fact of the **exile** caused the Israelites to think very hard about their relationship with God. God had given them the Promised Land so why did he allow them to be defeated and taken to another country, which did not even know God? Jeremiah had told the Israelites to accept exile as God's plan for them. They should settle down and learn to live in a godless, foreign country without the temple as a centre for their worship of the one true God. This message did not make Jeremiah popular. In fact he was imprisoned in a dry well. **You can read about what happened and how Jeremiah was rescued in Jeremiah chapter 38**.

The Book of Daniel describes how some Israelites worked hard in exile and even became important people. They had no temple but they began to meet in buildings which they called **synagogues** to worship God and to study the **scripture** more carefully. Learned men were becoming as important as the priests. These are the scribes and rabbis which we read about in the New Testament.

Ezekiel

As a young man, the prophet Ezekiel may have been amongst those who were taken across the desert from Judah to Babylon. He was a prophet to the Israelite exiles in Babylon. He explained why God had allowed the exile to happen and gave them hope for the future. Ezekiel had glorious visions of God and of a future temple with fresh water running from it to water the earth. **These visions are described in Ezekiel chapters 1 and 47**.

Facts!

The Babylonians had a long history but they became important in 626 BC when the father of Nebuchadnezzar rebuilt his capital city, Babylon. The walls of the city were so big and thick that chariots could drive along the top of them. It had a massive main gate and wonderful gardens which were recognised in their time as one of the Seven Wonders of the World.

Babylon was also a great centre of learning and culture. Sciences such as medicine, chemistry and mathematics were practised and law was studied. They were very religious people and worshipped many gods.

Did you know?

One psalm is a very sad song about the exiles in Babylon. They missed their homeland, and especially Jerusalem, so much that they could not respond to the demands of the Babylonians for a song about the city. Instead they hung their harps on willow trees by the river. Their suffering led them to have dreadful feelings of revenge against the Babylonians. **You will find their song in Psalm 137.**

WHAT WAS IT LIKE IN BABYLON?

The Israelites travelled over six hundred miles to Babylon, mostly across desert. Many would have had to walk. They exchanged life in a small, hilly country for the hot, flat plains of Babylonia. It was a land where most people worshipped many gods including the sun and moon and even the king himself. They had to learn a new language. People in Babylon wore fancy clothes with fringes and the men wore earrings, necklaces and armbands. Many things must have seemed very different for the Israelites.

Daniel

Daniel, Esther

The Book of Daniel tells the story of Daniel and his friends in the sixth century before Christ. Daniel was one of the Israelite exiles who had settled in Babylon.

Stories about Daniel

Daniel chapters 1 to 6 tell stories about Daniel and his friends, Hananiah, Mishael and Azariah, who were handsome and gifted young Israelite men. All four of these friends were given Babylonian names and were taken to the king's court to be trained as future leaders. They refused to eat the palace food, which would have been dedicated to the Babylonian gods. **You can read what happened in Daniel chapter 1, verses 8 to 16.**

> *"To these four young men God gave knowledge and understanding of all kinds of literature and learning. And Daniel could understand visions and dreams of all kinds."*
> *(Daniel chapter 1, verse 17 NIV)*

They faced many tests of their faith in God. When Daniel's three friends refused to bow down to the statue of the Babylonian king, Nebuchadnezzar, he threw them into a blazing furnace as punishment. An angel of God protected them. On another occasion, when evil men became jealous of Daniel, he was thrown into a den of lions. This time God's angel shut the mouths of the lions. **You will find this story in Daniel chapter 6.**

On two occasions Daniel was able to explain the meaning of King Nebuchadnezzar's dreams. On another famous occasion, some years later, Daniel explained some mysterious writing which appeared on the wall of King Belshazzar's palace. The writing was bad news since it warned the king that the Persians were going to invade and defeat Babylon, and that he himself would be killed.

The visions of Daniel

Chapters 7 to 12 of Daniel contain a series of strange visions. Some people think that these visions are about things which will happen just before Jesus comes back to earth a second time. Look up pages 102-103 to read more about this. Other people think that these visions are really about events which were happening when the book was written. **Look up Daniel, chapter 7, verses 1 to 14**. In this chapter Daniel describes future empires as strange and fierce animals. Then he writes about God himself, whom he calls the Ancient of Days, sitting upon his heavenly throne. He is far more powerful than all the nations and is really in control of everything. Daniel describes "one like a son of man" who was given power, glory and authority by God himself. Most Christians identify this figure with Jesus who called himself "the Son of Man".

Did you know?

Chapters 7 to 12 of the Book of Daniel are a kind of writing called "apocalyptic". It is also found in the book of Revelation in the New Testament. In some ways it is like science fiction. In this kind of writing, the writer may have strange visions about the future. Quite often he is writing secretly, in a kind of code, about things which were happening in his own day.

ESTHER

The Book of Esther is the story of a young Jewish girl who became the queen of the fearsome Persian king, Xerxes. She bravely used her new-found influence to help save her people, the Jews. Haman, who was the king's highest official, hated the Jews and was plotting to have them wiped out. The Jewish feast of Purim is still celebrated in memory of Esther's bravery.

Facts!

From now on we tend to speak about the "Jews" rather than Israelites. Those who went to Babylon were from Jerusalem and the southern kingdom of Judah. They were only the southern half of the original Israelites. After seventy years in Babylon, it was the Jews who returned home to Jerusalem and Judah.

Nehemiah, Ezra and the return from exile

Nehemiah, Ezra, Zechariah, Haggai

The Persian empire

The Persian king, Cyrus the Second, attacked Babylon in 539 BC, killing its king, Belshazzar. Cyrus allowed the Jews to begin the long return to Jerusalem. In 478 BC the Persians destroyed Babylon completely. The Persian court was very wealthy and many Jews were employed there and did very well.

The first to return home

In 537 BC a leader of the exiles called Zerubbabel (Ze-rub-a-bel) and a priest called Joshua returned with a group of other Jewish exiles to Jerusalem. Their first task was to start rebuilding the **temple,** starting with the altar. This is called the Second Temple, since Solomon's Temple had been destroyed by the Babylonians. They faced many enemies but Zerubbabel managed to make a start by offering sacrifices to God. Some years passed

before they made a new start on the temple and Zerubbabel was encouraged by the prophet Zechariah (Zek-a-rya) to see that it was God's work.

Ezra the priest

Ezra was sent to Jerusalem by the Persian king Artaxerxes (Art-a-zerx-ees) in 458 BC. His job was to organise those who had returned and to make sure they

obeyed God's Law. **Look up Nehemiah chapter 8 to read how Ezra gathered all the people together to hear the reading of God's word**. They made it a special day to be happy and all day the people had the words explained to them as they ate and enjoyed themselves.

Nehemiah rebuilds the walls of Jerusalem

King Artaxerxes later allowed his wine steward, Nehemiah, to return to Jerusalem as governor. First of all Nehemiah went to look around the city and to decide what needed to be done. Then he set about rebuilding the walls of the city. He organised the work so well that they finished it in fifty-two days. Nehemiah faced a great deal of opposition from the people who had settled in the land while the Jews were in exile. But Nehemiah was very determined and certain about what God had called him to do. Because of their enemies, Nehemiah told the builders to

carry a sword in one hand and to work with the other! That way they were always ready for an attack. He kept encouraging his people, saying "the joy of the Lord is your strength" (Nehemiah chapter 8, verse 10 NIV).

Facts!

The Book of Nehemiah is like a personal diary. Nehemiah himself tells us what he felt like when he went to ask the king's permission to go to Jerusalem. He tells us that he asked the king for timber to rebuild the city and an armed guard to escort him back to Jerusalem. He writes that the rebuilding was done by one hundred and fifty workers who ate one ox, six sheep and many chickens every day. Nehemiah was governor of Judah for twelve years.

Did you know?

Both Ezra and Nehemiah were very angry that the Jews in exile had begun to marry foreigners. They believed that God's people should remain separate from other nations. So they forced the people to get rid of their foreign partners and to find Jewish ones!

TWO PROPHETS

Between 520 and 516 BC, the two prophets who encouraged the returning exiles were Zechariah and Haggai. Haggai promised that this second temple would be even greater than that built by Solomon. They were very different characters. Whilst Haggai was very plain and straightforward in his words, Zechariah saw colourful and exciting visions. You can compare them if you look up their books towards the end of the Old Testament.

A VERSE TO REMEMBER
"God promised, 'Very old people with walking sticks will once again sit around in Jerusalem, while boys and girls play in the streets.'"
(Zechariah chapter 8, verses 4 to 5 CEV)

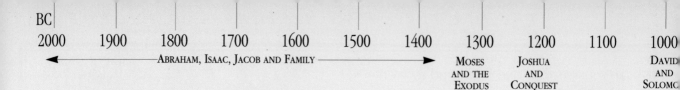

BC									
2000	1900	1800	1700	1600	1500	1400	1300	1200	1100	1000

◄———— ABRAHAM, ISAAC, JACOB AND FAMILY ————►

MOSES AND THE EXODUS — JOSHUA AND CONQUEST — DAVID AND SOLOMO

After the exile

Returning or staying?

After the return from exile there are about four hundred years which the Bible tells us very little about. Many thousands of Jews returned from exile. The temple and the city walls of Jerusalem were rebuilt.

Quite a number of Jews decided to remain where they were. Some (like Daniel) stayed in Persia. Some had gone to Egypt. Others had gone to Rome and Athens and other great cities. Wherever they went, they built synagogues. These were meeting places, rather like churches, where Jewish people could meet to pray, study the Bible and worship God.

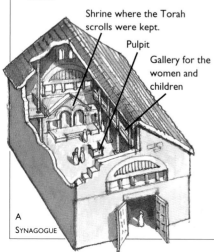

Shrine where the Torah scrolls were kept.

Pulpit

Gallery for the women and children

A SYNAGOGUE

Stories and festivals

Their Bible was what Christians now call the Old Testament. The Old Testament had been written down mostly in Hebrew, the language of the Jews. But during this time, it was

THE EMPIRE OF ALEXANDER THE GREAT

translated into the Greek language. This was very important because Greek was understood by many more people in those days, rather like English is today.

Jews who remained in exile tried to get to the temple in Jerusalem every year for the main festivals of Passover, Pentecost and Tabernacles. These took place in spring, summer and

autumn when Jerusalem was crowded with people whom we would describe as pilgrims.

Invaders and conquerors

Although the Bible does not give us information about this time, other books fill in what happened in the four hundred years before Jesus was born. Back home in Israel, life was hard. In fact time after time invaders came and took away their freedom. The first important ones to do this were the Greeks. They had become a great power under one of the greatest soldiers the world has ever known. He was Alexander

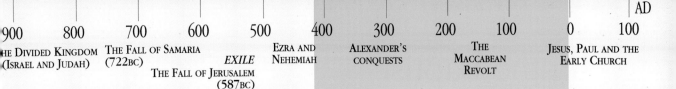

| 900 | 800 | 700 | 600 | 500 | 400 | 300 | 200 | 100 | 0 | 100 | AD |

THE DIVIDED KINGDOM (ISRAEL AND JUDAH)

THE FALL OF SAMARIA (722BC)

EXILE

THE FALL OF JERUSALEM (587BC)

EZRA AND NEHEMIAH

ALEXANDER'S CONQUESTS

THE MACCABEAN REVOLT

JESUS, PAUL AND THE EARLY CHURCH

the Great. Alexander lived for only thirty-three years but in that time conquered all the land between Greece and India, including Israel. Alexander's conquest is very important because it spread Greek learning and government over a very large area.

The Jews often rebelled against their conquerors. Their most famous leader was Judas Maccabeus (the Hammer). In 164BC, after a number of fierce battles, Judas managed to drive the Greek rulers out of Jerusalem and the temple. He was a great hero and Jewish people today remember him at the Feast of Hannukah, just before

Christmas, when they light candles and celebrate. Sadly Judas was not always a wise ruler. In the years following his death, members of his family became rulers. They quarrelled with each other and plotted and sometimes murdered each other.

The Romans

It is hardly surprising that Israel was soon conquered again, this time by the Romans, who had overcome the power of Greece. The Romans had an excellent army and gradually conquered all the world known to them. It was the Roman general Pompey who rode into Jerusalem to take the city for the Romans. The Romans never understood the Jews and the Jews hated the Romans. They began to hope more and more for a coming deliverer, whom they called the Messiah.

This brings us to the time of the New Testament. In his gospel, Luke writes - "In those days Caesar Augustus issued a decree that a census should be taken of the entire Roman world" (Luke chapter 2, verse 1 NIV). The Romans were still

Facts!

Surprisingly even quite a lot of Jews preferred to read in Greek because they no longer understood Hebrew quite so well. At this time a number of extra books were added to the Old Testament which we call the Apocrypha. These books, such as 1 and 2 Maccabees or the Wisdom of Solomon, appear in some Bibles but not all.

Did you know?

Even in Israel, Greek schools were built and children were taught how to think and act like Greeks. They were encouraged to worship Greek gods and give up the way of life which was especially Jewish. A great many Jews were very unhappy about this and refused

in charge, but one baby, born in Bethlehem during this census, was to be "King of Kings, and Lord of Lords". The kingdom of Jesus was a very different kind of kingdom which would never end.

POMPEY'S DREADFUL DEED

Pompey cared nothing for Jewish ways or religion and went straight into the most holy place in the temple to see what was there. This was a great insult to the Jews, because only the High Priest was allowed there.

John the Baptist
Luke chapter 3, verses 1 to 20

A man like Elijah

John the Baptist was a cousin of Jesus. He was also a fiery prophet and spent much of his time preaching in the desert where people came to listen to him. He brought God's powerful message to the Jews. People recognised him as being just like Elijah, the Old Testament prophet. But not everyone liked him. The Jewish king, Herod, was his enemy. John described himself as

> *"the voice of one shouting in the desert: Make a straight path for the Lord to travel!"*
> *(John chapter 1, verse 23 GNB)*

And that was his job – to prepare the way for Jesus.

John's message

John's message can be summed up in one word – "repent". This meant that he wanted people to change their ways and live better lives. He believed that God was about to send his special messenger, called the **Messiah,** into the world and that people needed to get ready to receive him. He told people to share their belongings with the poor and he told tax collectors to be fair. He told soldiers to be happy with the pay they received. **You can read what he said in Luke chapter 3, verses 1 to 20.**

The baptiser

John's nickname was "the baptiser". If people wanted to repent and confess their sins, they could go to John by the River Jordan. He called them into the river where he drenched them with water. Just as the water made them clean, so God would forgive or "wash away" their sins.

His death

One of John's enemies was King Herod who was living with his brother's wife, Herodias. John told Herod that this was wrong. So Herod put John in prison to silence him and Herodias tried to find a way to have John killed. In prison, John had doubts about Jesus and sent some of his followers to ask Jesus if he was really the Messiah after all. Jesus reminded John of the miracles and preaching he had done.

One evening, at a party, Herod was so pleased with the dancing of Herodias'

daughter, Salome, that he promised to give her whatever she asked for. Herodias told her to ask for the head of John the Baptist. **Look up Mark chapter 6, verses 14 to 29 for this story.**

Did you know?

John's father, Zechariah, became dumb for some months before John was born. When the time came to name the baby, Zechariah wrote "His name is John" on a writing tablet. Writing tablets were shallow wooden boxes with wax at the bottom. A sharp pen was used to write in the wax. Afterwards, it could be smoothed over and used again.

CLOTHES AND FOOD

John's clothing would make everyone think of Elijah, who was also a prophet from the desert. He wore rough clothes made out of camel hair, fastened with a leather belt and ate wild honey and locusts, insects which were common in desert areas.

A VERSE TO REMEMBER

"Jesus added, 'John is greater than anyone who has ever lived. But the one who is least in the Kingdom of God is greater than John.'"
(Luke chapter 7, verse 28 GNB)

The early years of Jesus

Matthew chapters 1 to 4;
Luke chapters 1 to 3

Jesus is born

Jesus was born in Bethlehem. As the prophet Micah had predicted:

> *"Bethlehem in the land of Judea,*
> *you are very important among the*
> *towns of Judea.*
> *From your town will come a leader,*
> *who will be like a shepherd for my people*
> *Israel."*
> *· (Matthew chapter 2, verse 6 CEV)*

The gospel writers, Matthew and Luke, tell us the story of the birth of Jesus. It is Matthew who tells us about the wise men who followed the star to Bethlehem to find the baby. He also tells us how the family had to escape to Egypt. Luke tells us how an angel told Mary about the child she was to bear, and more angels appeared to shepherds and told them where to find the child.

His childhood

We know very little about Jesus' childhood, but we do know that, when he was very young, he became a refugee in order to escape from the cruelty of King Herod who feared that a new king had been born who might replace him. He grew up in the town of Nazareth and probably helped Joseph who was a carpenter.

John baptises Jesus

When Jesus was about thirty, his first public action was to go to be baptised by John the Baptist in the River Jordan. This is not because he thought he was a sinner, but because he wanted to show that he approved of what John was doing. As Jesus was being baptised, a voice from heaven said, "This is my own dear son, and I am pleased with him." (Matthew chapter 3, verse 17 CEV)

The devil tests Jesus

Straight after his baptism, Jesus went into the desert and was tested by the devil three times. The **devil** first encouraged Jesus to turn stones into bread, because he was hungry. Then he challenged Jesus to prove he was the Son of God by throwing himself off the highest part of the temple. Thirdly, the devil offered Jesus power if he would worship him. Jesus, of course, refused to do any of these things. **You can read about how he did this in Matthew chapter 4, verses 1 to 11.**

Facts!

When Jewish boys were about five they began to study the Law and at about thirteen years of age, they were held responsible for obeying its commands. They were regarded as "grown up". When he was twelve, Jesus had already shown how wise he was when he talked with the teachers in the temple. **Read about this in Luke chapter 2, verses 41 to 52.** Nowadays Jewish boys celebrate becoming an adult at a ceremony called a bar-mitzvah.

DISCIPLES

Large crowds followed Jesus, but he chose only twelve men as his followers or disciples. Most of them were from Galilee like Jesus. Some were fishermen. Matthew was a tax-collector, working for the Roman government. Simon is described as a freedom fighter. They followed Jesus everywhere, listened to his teaching and studied the way he lived. Later on, after Jesus went back to heaven, they were called "apostles" and were responsible for telling people the truth about Jesus.

Facts!

THE TWELVE DISCIPLES
Simon Peter, the leader
Andrew, Simon Peter's brother
John, the son of Zebedee
James, John's brother
Philip
Bartholomew
Thomas, the doubter
Matthew, the tax-collector
James, the son of Alphaeus
Thaddaeus
Simon, the freedom fighter
Judas Iscariot, the traitor

Did you know?

Angels are God's special messengers who appear from time to time in the Bible. They were especially important at the time of Jesus' birth, telling people, like Mary and Joseph, what was going to happen. We are not told what they look like and they are never said to have wings! But they are clearly very frightening. They usually begin by telling people "Don't be frightened".

And did you know that the Bible never tells us how many wise men came to visit the baby Jesus? It only tells us that they brought three kinds of gift: gold, frankincense and myrrh.

Jesus the teacher
Matthew 5-7

Jesus wasn't a trained rabbi or teacher and his job was being a carpenter, not a teacher. Often he criticised the rabbis and the Pharisees and said that their way of understanding the Old Testament and the Law was wrong. This made him a lot of enemies.

A great teacher

Ordinary people loved listening to Jesus. His teaching was interesting and was about things that were familiar to them like sheep and money. He told many stories, called parables. These stories made people think and they would often have a punch-line or a twist at the end to drive his point home. Two of the most famous are the Parable of the Good Samaritan and the Parable of the Lost Son. **You can read them in Luke chapter 10, verses 30 to 37 and chapter 15, verses 11 to 32.** Sometimes Jesus said things which must have made people laugh, like the idea of a camel going through the eye of a needle. Sometimes he was very serious and warned people that they needed to obey God's commands.

The Kingdom of God

Jesus' main message was that the Kingdom of God had come. He wasn't saying that a new country had arrived but that he had come to show people how God wanted them to live. They were to think of God as their king. He told many parables about the kingdom of God. Some of them promise a future time when God will be King over the whole world.

What Jesus taught about himself

Jesus often called God his father. This is one reason why people began to think of him as God's Son. He even taught his disciples to pray the Lord's Prayer, which begins "Our father in heaven". Jesus preferred to call himself the Son of Man. Jesus also talked frequently about the suffering he would experience. He couldn't avoid it. Indeed God wanted him to go through with it. It was part of God's plan that Jesus would die on the cross.

THE SERMON ON THE MOUNT

The Sermon on the Mount is possibly the best known part of Jesus' teaching. **You can read it in Matthew chapters 5 to 7.** The Lord's Prayer is there and a lot of famous verses like "Look at the birds flying around: they do not sow seeds, gather a harvest and put it in barns; yet your Father in heaven takes care of them! Aren't you worth much more than birds?" (Matthew chapter 6, verse 26 GNB).

PHARISEES

The Pharisees were also teachers. They wanted people to live in a way which pleased God. So they tried to obey in every detail the laws that God had given to Moses. They also made up a lot of extra rules to make sure that they didn't risk breaking any of God's laws. Jesus argued with them a great deal about these extra laws which only managed to make life very difficult for ordinary people. Jesus also criticised them for pretending to be better than they were.

The Pharisees wore small boxes, attached to their forehead and arm, which contained part of the Law. They were called phylacteries.

WHAT THEY SAID ABOUT JESUS

"The large crowd enjoyed listening to Jesus teach." (Mark chapter 12, verse 37 CEV)

"Everyone was amazed at his teaching. He taught with authority, and not like the teachers of the Law of Moses." (Mark chapter 1, verse 22 CEV)

"Simon Peter answered, 'Lord, there is no-one else that we can go to! Your words give eternal life'" (John chapter 6, verse 68 CEV)

Did you know?

Parables are clever and memorable stories about everyday life which also tell us something about God. The Parable of the Sower, in Mark chapter 4 verses 1 to 20, shows the different ways in which people respond to hearing God's message. The Parable of the Two House Builders, in Matthew chapter 7, verses 24 to 27, tells us to build our lives on the rock of Jesus' teaching.

The Sower

The Prodigal Son

The Good Samaritan

The Two Builders

Jesus the healer

Jesus - a worker of miracles

Jesus did many miracles. People often came to him because they had heard this. Many of them were sick and hoped that he would make them better. Others probably just wanted to see what he might do. The Pharisees asked him to do miracles as a sign which would prove to them that he was indeed the **Messiah.** Jesus refused.

Jesus brings healing

On one occasion some men brought a friend who was unable to walk. They made a hole in the roof of the house where Jesus was teaching and lowered the man down in front of Jesus. Jesus knew that this man needed to have his sins forgiven, so he forgave him. Then Jesus healed the man. **You can read this story in Mark chapter 2, verses 1 to 12.** Jesus also healed blind people, deaf people, people who couldn't walk, people suffering from leprosy and so on.

Jesus defeats the devil

Sometimes Jesus met people whose lives were under the devil's control. This made them seem mad. They couldn't control themselves. On these occasions Jesus ordered the devil to leave these people alone. This is called exorcism (eggs-or-sisum). Jesus was fighting against the powers of evil and showed that his power was far greater. **One story about exorcism can be found in Mark chapter 5, verses 1 to 20.**

Jesus defeats death

There are three stories about times when Jesus brought people back from the dead. Two were men and one was a twelve-year-old daughter of a man called Jairus. One of the men, named Lazarus, had already been in the tomb for four days. But Jesus called him and Lazarus came out still wrapped up in his grave clothes. **You can read this story in John chapter 11, verses 1 to 44.**

The meaning of miracles

Sometimes Jesus did miracles which had a deeper meaning. On one occasion a crowd of 5,000 families followed him out into the countryside, far from any town. They got hungry and Jesus fed them, using just five loaves and two little fishes. Thoughtful Jews might remember how God had miraculously fed their ancestors in the desert in the days of Moses.

MIRACLES

God is always working in his world. He makes things happen like the beginning of a new day or the flowers growing in springtime. The Bible tells us that God keeps the whole universe going all of the time. Sometimes he does special things which we don't understand and which seem impossible. These would include raising a person from the dead or making a sick person well. We call these things "miracles". But God is not breaking any laws of science. He is simply doing things in a way which we don't understand.

Facts!

Jesus did many miracles though the Gospels don't record all of them. But we do have fifteen stories about when Jesus healed people, six stories about when he drove the devil out of people's lives, three stories about when he raised the dead and eight stories about when he did other miracles like walking on the water or feeding the five thousand.

Did you know?

Not everyone was impressed by the miracles Jesus did. The Pharisees, for example, accused him of doing miracles by the power of the devil. This was a very serious charge and implied that Jesus was a disciple of the devil. Jesus described what they said as the "unforgivable sin". They were deliberately refusing to see God the Father at work in the ministry of Jesus.

Jesus and people

The man who loved people
Jesus said that the two most important commandments are to love God and to love your neighbour. **You can find this teaching in Mark chapter 12, verses 29 to 31.** Jesus is the only person who has ever perfectly loved God and other people.

The friend of sinners and outcasts
Jesus was described as "the friend of sinners". "Sinners" were thought to be the worst people possible, but, if they asked for forgiveness, Jesus forgave their sins. The Pharisees were very careful about who they spoke to and who they ate with. So they were very shocked that Jesus ate with **tax collectors** and sinners. One of his disciples, Matthew, left his job as a tax collector and became a follower of Jesus.

You can read this story in Matthew chapter 9, verses 9 to 12.
In the time of Jesus, people who had leprosy were outcasts. Other people would have kept well away from them. But Jesus not only spoke to them but actually touched and healed them as well.

Rich friends, poor friends
Jesus had friends who were poor. He and his disciples travelled a great deal and had no homes or regular source of food. But Jesus also had some friends who were well off. Some wealthy people provided things for him and his disciples. He loved people whether they were rich or poor. **In Mark chapter 10, verses 17 to 31 you can read the story of a rich young man.** This person had lived a very good life but Jesus was very tough with him. He said that the man should sell everything he had and give it to the poor, and come and follow Jesus. Sadly the man was not prepared to give up everything for Jesus.

Pharisees and ordinary people
The Pharisees disliked Jesus from the very beginning and were soon plotting to destroy him. He had many arguments with them and was not afraid to point out where they were simply pretending to be good. The crowds of people, who followed Jesus around, were very unreliable and easily changed their minds. At first they loved Jesus and followed him about. He taught them and they wanted him to be king. But Jesus was not willing to be the kind of king they wanted and the crowd soon began to hate him. At the end they cried out, "Crucify him!"

Did you know?

At the time of Jesus, men looked down on women and thought they were inferior. But Jesus spoke with women and treated them with respect, like real people. This was very unusual in his day. **You can read about two women who met Jesus in John chapter 4, verses 4 to 42 and Luke chapter 7, verses 36 to 50.** There were quite a few women among his followers and they helped provide him with food and hospitality. At the cross, women stayed with Jesus until he died. It was women who first discovered the empty tomb and saw the risen Jesus.

NICODEMUS

Not all of the Pharisees disliked Jesus. **In John chapter 3, verses 1 to 21, you can read about Nicodemus.** He was a Pharisee who came one night to talk about religion with Jesus. Jesus told Nicodemus how a person could be "born again" and begin a completely new life with God. Nicodemus did not become an open follower of Jesus, but at the end of Jesus' life he came forward to help with burying Jesus. **Look up John chapter 19, verse 39.**

Facts!

The Jews hated the Romans because they had invaded their land and made it part of their empire. The Jews were often rebelling against them. But Jesus taught people not to use violence and to pay their taxes to the Roman government. He showed that he cared for Romans too by healing a Roman soldier's servant. Jesus respected the man's faith in him and said that many such people would be in heaven. **Read this story in Matthew chapter 8, verses 5 to 13.**

The death of Jesus

Matthew 21,26-27; Mark 11,14-15; Luke 19,22-23; John 18-19

Arrival in Jerusalem

Jesus entered Jerusalem to the sound of cheering and celebration. It was the Passover festival and the crowd was in holiday mood. They also wanted to see this preacher who had caused such excitement. When he visited the temple, Jesus was shocked to see the way traders were doing business and chased them out. Business had taken over where prayer and worship should have been in people's minds.

Betrayal!

One of Jesus' disciples, Judas Iscariot, had already accepted money to betray Jesus to his enemies. Judas still went to share the Passover meal with Jesus and the other disciples. Peter, the leading disciple, was shocked to be told by Jesus that he would deny that he had ever known Jesus. After they had eaten, they went out to a garden called Gethsemane (Geth-sem-any) on the Mount of Olives, where Jesus prayed.

Arrested and tried!

Judas had left during the Passover meal, but came to the garden with a crowd to arrest Jesus. Jesus had two trials. First the Jewish court, the Sanhedrin, found him guilty of saying that he was God. In Jewish Law, this was called **blasphemy** and the punishment was death. But the Romans didn't allow the Jews to execute anyone, so Jesus had to be tried before the Roman governor Pontius Pilot. Under pressure, Pilate gave way. Jesus was to be crucified even though no-one could prove he had done anything wrong.

Meanwhile, Peter *did* in fact deny Jesus three times, just as Jesus had said he would. Peter soon realised he had done wrong and wept bitterly. After the resurrection Jesus forgave him completely. But Judas never did ask for forgiveness and, in the end, took his own life.

Jesus is crucified

It was common for soldiers and those watching crucifixions to make fun of the victim. This was true in Jesus' case. He was whipped, spat at, laughed at and stripped naked. He was made to wear a crown made of sharp thorns. Then he was crucified between two criminals. Normally it took people a long time to die, but Jesus had already been beaten up, so it took only about six hours. It was getting dark and the Jewish rest day, the Sabbath, began then – not in the morning – so they took Jesus' body down from the cross.

Did you know?

The Last Supper was a Passover celebration, and was Jesus' last meal with his disciples. During the supper, he explained that he was going to die. He also explained the meaning of his death by breaking bread and pouring out wine. The breaking of bread was a picture of what would happen to his body on the cross. The wine would remind them that he bled on the cross for them. Jesus encouraged his followers to break bread and drink wine to remember his death. Christians still do this today.

Facts!

Crucifixion was the way that the Romans executed common criminals or freedom fighters. It was quite common for people to see naked bodies hanging dead or dying on crosses at the side of the road. For a Jew it was especially shameful to be stripped naked and in the Old Testament there was a curse on anyone who suffered death by hanging from a tree like the cross.

WHY DID JESUS DIE?

At Passover Jews killed and ate a lamb. It reminded them of when they had escaped from Egypt hundreds of years before. On that occasion the angel of death had *passed over* the houses where the blood of a lamb had been sprinkled on the door frame. They also believed that this lamb paid the price for their wrongdoing. Jesus is sometimes called the "Lamb of God" because he also was killed at Passover time. Christians believe that he died instead of us for all the wrong things we have done.

The resurrection of Jesus

Matthew 28, Mark 16, Luke 24, John 20-22

The death of Jesus

Jesus died on the cross. The Romans sent men around to check that victims were really dead. If there was any sign of life, they broke their legs, which finished people off very quickly. But they didn't need to do that with Jesus though they did stick a spear in his side. Jesus' followers quickly took his body and laid it in a tomb belonging to Joseph of Arimathea, a rich follower of Jesus. They had to do this quickly because the Sabbath was about to begin and no Jew would handle a dead body then.

The tomb

Joseph's tomb probably belonged to his family and was cut into the rock, like most Jewish tombs. Jesus' body was laid on a slab. Around the edges of the tomb there would usually be the bones of other people who had been placed there after death. But this was a new tomb. Nobody knows nowadays exactly where Jesus' tomb is. It was quickly forgotten, which is not surprising because Jesus came alive again. The tomb wasn't important any more. As the angels said to the women, "Why do you look for the living among the dead?" (Luke chapter 24, verse 5 NIV).

Early on Easter Sunday

Very early in the morning it was the women who went to the tomb to put ointments and spices on the body. They were astonished to find the body gone and just the burial cloths which had been wrapped around it left behind. When angels told them that Jesus was alive, they hurried back to tell the other disciples. The disciples didn't believe them. In the end Peter went to look for himself and was very puzzled.

Meeting the risen Lord

Jesus had risen from the dead! He appeared to several of his disciples over a period of about forty days. At first they found it difficult to recognise him, but it was eventually clear to them that this was the same Jesus they had known and loved. He invited them to eat with him and encouraged Thomas to feel the wounds in his hands and side to be sure that it really was him and that he was not some kind of ghost.

Did you know?

Nowadays, in most countries, it is common for people either to bury dead bodies in the earth or else to burn them. In Israel the bodies were placed in tombs in the side of rocks. Soon, in such a warm climate, all that was left were the bones. When that had happened, the bones were gathered up and placed in a container.

THIS IS IMPORTANT!

Christians believe that Jesus rose from the dead. He was not a spirit or a ghost even though he was able to pass through doors and move more easily from place to place. He ate and spoke normally with his disciples. This is the basis of the Christian belief that we too will be raised from the dead one day. Paul describes Jesus as the firstfruits of a harvest that is sure to come.

THE FINAL RESURRECTION

Many at the time of Jesus believed that God would raise all people from the dead at the very end of time. God would then judge them according to what they had done. What they didn't expect was that God would raise one person in advance of all the rest. But this shows how special Jesus and his work actually were.

A VERSE TO REMEMBER

The angel said, "He is not here; he has risen, just as he said. Come and see the place where he lay." (Matthew chapter 28, verse 6 NIV)

BC										
2000	1900	1800	1700	1600	1500	1400	1300	1200	1100	1000

◄————— Abraham, Isaac, Jacob and Family —————►

Moses
and the
Exodus

Joshua
and
Conquest

David
and
Solomo[n]

The Gospels and their writers
Matthew, Mark, Luke and John

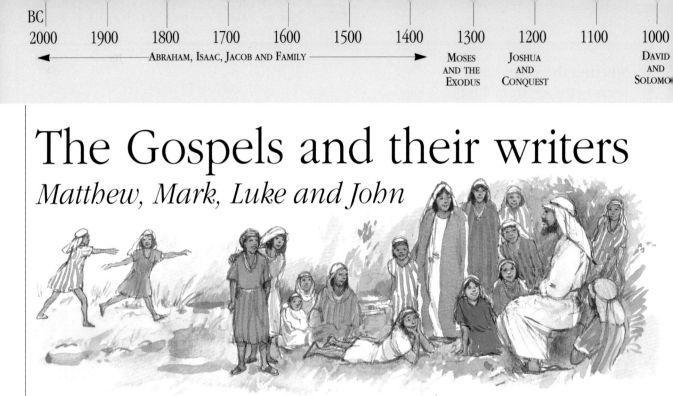

Four gospels, one Jesus

The gospels tell us about the life of Jesus. They don't tell us much about his childhood or his work as a carpenter. They tell us about the last three years of his life when he did his most important work as a teacher and healer. Why are there four gospels? The gospels are like four portraits of the same person, painted by different artists. Each gospel shows us something different about Jesus. Matthew, Mark and Luke are very similar to each other. John tells many different stories and includes a lot more of what Jesus taught at the Last Supper.

Matthew

It is quite possible that it was Matthew the tax collector, one of the twelve disciples, who wrote the first gospel.

Matthew includes a lot of Jesus' teaching such as the "Sermon on the Mount" (see page 79). Matthew was probably writing especially for Jewish Christians and he includes a lot of Old Testament quotations because he wants to show that the writers of the Old Testament were looking ahead to Jesus.

Mark

Mark himself was a missionary companion of Paul and the cousin of Barnabas (see page 99). The gospel of Mark is the shortest of the gospels. It is fast-moving and very exciting. He uses the word "immediately" more than forty times in his stories. Mark loves to tell stories and doesn't report very much of Jesus' teaching. He gives us a very full account of the trial and

crucifixion of Jesus. Mark may have got some of his stories from the apostle Peter. Certainly Mark's gospel reflects something of Peter's character in its eagerness.

Luke

Luke may well have been a doctor and another of Paul's travelling companions. He was almost certainly a Gentile and his gospel contains many stories and teaching about

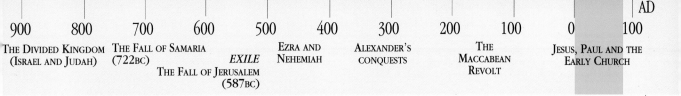

| 900 | 800 | 700 | 600 | 500 | 400 | 300 | 200 | 100 | 0 | 100 | AD |

THE DIVIDED KINGDOM (ISRAEL AND JUDAH) THE FALL OF SAMARIA (722BC) *EXILE* EZRA AND NEHEMIAH ALEXANDER'S CONQUESTS THE MACCABEAN REVOLT JESUS, PAUL AND THE EARLY CHURCH

THE FALL OF JERUSALEM (587BC)

non-Jews. Luke also records a lot of Jesus' teaching about riches and poverty. He includes many of the best-known parables of Jesus such as the Lost Son in chapter 15 and the Good Samaritan in chapter 10.

John - the different gospel

John and his brother James were called "sons of thunder" by Jesus. John's gospel has a lot of stories about Jesus which do not appear in the other three. It includes some famous stories like the changing of water into wine in chapter 2, the healing of the man born blind in chapter 9 and the raising to life of Lazarus from the dead in chapter 11.

Facts!

Jesus lived in the area known as Galilee. A number of different languages were probably spoken. Roman soldiers might speak Latin or Greek. The Jewish people would speak either Aramaic or Hebrew. Jesus probably spoke Aramaic most of the time. All of the New Testament was written in Greek which was the language most used at the time, rather like English is today. Most people probably spoke several languages.

Hebrew writing   Greek writing

TRANSLATION

The Old Testament was translated into Greek nearly two hundred years before Jesus was born (see page 72). The gospels were first written in Greek, so the words of Jesus, which were probably spoken in Aramaic, were translated. See pages 106-107 for more about Bible translation.

A VERSE TO REMEMBER

"God loved the people of this world so much that he gave his only Son, so that everyone who has faith in him will have eternal life and never really die." (John chapter 3, verse 16 CEV)

Did you know?

Nobody can be quite sure when the gospels were first written down. Stories about Jesus were first passed around by word of mouth. Mark was probably the first gospel written down in about 60 AD. Matthew, Luke and John may have been written in the 80s or 90s.

Life in Jesus' time

Jews and Romans

At the time when Jesus was born, the Romans ruled most of the Mediterranean world. They had not yet conquered Britain but had reached France and most of North Africa. In 66 BC Israel became part of the Roman province of Syria and was controlled by the Roman army. Although kings like Herod were not Roman, they had to obey what the Romans commanded. Most Jewish people disliked this and some were prepared to fight the Romans. Revolt was in the air. The Romans appointed a governor, such as Pontius Pilate, to maintain security and public order. He also collected taxes and was a kind of judge in legal disputes.

Pharisees and Sadducees

The Pharisees were religious leaders. They wanted people to live in a way which pleased God. So they tried to obey the laws that God had given to Moses in every detail. They also made up a lot of extra rules to make sure that they didn't risk breaking any of God's laws. Jesus argued with them a great deal about these extra laws which only managed to make life very difficult for ordinary people. For example, the Pharisees criticised Jesus for healing people on the Sabbath. They

didn't want people to do anything at all on that day.

The Sadducees were mostly politicians who were connected to the temple in Jerusalem. They were very important in the Sanhedrin, the ruling body which decided everyday matters.

Galilee, Samaria and Jerusalem

Jesus grew up in Galilee, in the north of Israel. When he went to Jerusalem for the festivals, possibly three times a year, he had to walk. This was quite usual because very few people had donkeys or other animals. When Jews travelled from north to south, they usually went around a long way to avoid Samaria which lay partly in between. This was because the Jews and Samaritans did not like each other. Jesus told a famous parable about a good Samaritan, which must have surprised his hearers. **Look up Luke chapter 10, verses 30 to 37.**

Education

Schools like we have today were not known in Bible times. Children were taught many things by their parents at home, like a trade or business. Boys might also be taught to read and recite in the synagogue. This education would be mostly concerned with "right and wrong". Religion was the most important subject. Sometimes a famous rabbi, or teacher, would have his own school, but only for boys. Girls were taught housework and how to read by their mothers at home.

Facts!

There were three kinds of money in Palestine. First, there was the official Roman money like the silver denarius which carried the head of the emperor. Then there was Greek money like the silver drachma which was much used by traders. Lastly, Jewish coins existed, which were mostly made out of bronze. A carpenter like Jesus, or fishermen like some of the disciples, may have used all three kinds of money.

Roman

Greek

Jewish

HOUSES

Most ordinary houses were small and built close together, often inside cities with walls all around. People might have houses made of rough stones or mud bricks with walls up to one metre thick. Floors were made of clay. The low wooden doors were kept open to let in the light. There were usually no windows on the ground floor, and an outside staircase led to a flat roof where people might sleep in warm weather. Houses were often used as workshops. Sometimes animals, like oxen or donkeys, were kept in the houses.

FOOD

Most people in Jesus' time ate very little meat except at the feasts of Passover, Pentecost and Tabernacles (see page 41). Fish was more common. Bread made of wheat or barley was the basic food. Grapes and figs were enjoyed and olives were eaten with bread. They also ate beans, onions, leeks and lentils, which were boiled or cooked in oil. Insects such as locusts and grasshoppers were also eaten. The Jews had very strict laws about what they were allowed to eat (see page 40).

The first Christians

Acts 1-15

The twelve apostles

Forty days after the resurrection, Jesus left his disciples and returned to heaven. This is called the ascension. **You can read about it in Acts chapter 1.** From now on the disciples are called "apostles". The apostles were men who had been with Jesus throughout his ministry and who could swear to the truth of the resurrection. They were also missionaries who took the message about Jesus from Jerusalem to all over the world. This was Jesus' final instruction to them. **Look up Matthew chapter 28, verses 19 and 20.**

Stephen and his friends

At the feast of Pentecost, many Jews came from foreign cities to worship God in Jerusalem. Stephen was possibly one of them and he believed the good news about Jesus. He spoke out about his faith in Jesus and the Jewish leaders arrested him. He was stoned to death. A man called Saul watched him die. This Saul became

the apostle Paul (see page 94). Christians began to suffer terribly. Philip was one of many Christians who escaped from Jerusalem taking the message about Jesus with them. They began to talk about their faith with people who were not Jews.

Peter and Cornelius

Simon Peter was the leader of the apostles. One day he had a vision in which God told him to go to the house of a Roman soldier called Cornelius to tell him about Jesus. This was a great step for Peter to take, since Jews and Gentiles did not mix. Cornelius became the first Gentile Christian.

James

The church in Jerusalem was completely Jewish. The leader was James, who may have been the brother of Jesus. There were even some Pharisees who became Christians. They found it very difficult to see how Gentiles could become the people of God without becoming Jews. In about the year 49 AD, there was a meeting called the Council of Jerusalem to decide what to do about all of these Gentile Christians. They decided to welcome the Gentiles. One of the chief members of this council was a man named Paul. You can read more about him about on pages 94-99.

GROWTH OF THE CHURCH

The number of believers in Jesus grew very rapidly and spread out all over the Roman empire especially in the great cities like Rome, Antioch, Alexandria and Ephesus. The first Christians were all Jews but very soon the number of Gentile Christians became much greater. They nearly always faced opposition from both Jews and pagans. But this never put them off and, within three hundred years, Christianity had become the religion of the Roman emperor Constantine.

THE LETTERS OF PETER

Two letters in the New Testament are named after Peter. His first letter is to Gentile Christians in modern day Turkey. These Christians were facing terrible persecution and Peter wrote to encourage them. He reminds them that they are the true people of God. In his second letter, Peter writes about what it means to live a holy life and about God's plan for the future.

Did you know?

The feast of Pentecost is forty days after Easter. It is also known as Whit Sunday. Christians remember that it was at Pentecost that God first sent the Holy Spirit to his disciples. The **Holy Spirit** came like a great wind and tongues of fire seemed to rest upon each believer as they began to speak in other languages. **You can read about this in Acts chapter 2, verses 1 to 13.** Pentecost is the birthday of the church.

THE LETTER OF JAMES

We have one letter from James in the New Testament. It is very practical and covers subjects like not being proud and resisting temptation. James criticises the rich and orders them to look after the poor. He points out that we show our faith by what we do and the way we speak. **Look up James chapter 3, verses 4 to 8.**

Paul becomes a Christian

Acts 9-15, Galatians 1-2

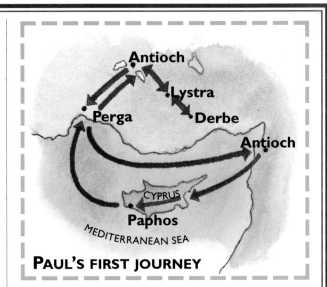

PAUL'S FIRST JOURNEY

The man from Tarsus

Saul, who became known as Paul, didn't grow up in Jerusalem. He came from Tarsus in the east of present-day Turkey. But he was a Jew and may well have gone to study in Jerusalem when he got a bit older. He was a Pharisee (see page 79) and studied under famous teachers. His commitment to what he believed made him think that Jesus and his followers should be wiped out.

Saul becomes a follower of Jesus

On his final trip to arrest followers of Jesus in Damascus, Saul met the risen Lord Jesus in a blinding light from heaven. He fell to the ground and was blinded. A voice said, "I am Jesus... I am the one you are so cruel to." (Acts chapter 9, verse 5 CEV). Saul was taken to Damascus where a man called Ananias looked after him and explained to him that God had chosen him to be an apostle and that he would suffer many things as he took the message about Jesus to Gentile people. So he became one of the most important Christians that have ever lived.

Paul becomes a missionary

Some time later, the church in Antioch decided to send out missionaries to spread the message about Jesus. They sent off Barnabas, Saul and others to Cyprus and Galatia, in what is now southern Turkey, to begin what is usually called "the first missionary journey". **You can read all about it in Acts 13 and 14.** From this point on, Saul, who was a Roman citizen, became known as Paul, which was his Roman name.

Sorting out problems

It wasn't long before problems arose. Outsiders came to teach the churches in Galatia that Gentile Christians needed to be circumcised, like the Jews, in order to be the true people of God (see page 23). Paul was very angry and argued strongly against this. He wrote the letter called Galatians to explain that Gentiles could become Christians without being circumcised or obeying the Law in the way that Jews did. But this problem kept cropping up for Paul and he had to deal with it in more letters later on.

JEWS AND GENTILES

The Jews believed they were God's special people. They tended to look down on everyone else who were called Gentiles. They thought that the Gentiles were not special to God. The Gentiles did not obey God's laws and did many things which the Jews found unpleasant like eating meat with blood left in it. The Jews found it very difficult to believe that God could want the Gentiles to become Christians. Unless, of course, they first became Jews!

WHAT PAUL PREACHED

Paul realised that God wanted even the Gentiles to become Christians. He also understood that it was unnecessary for them to become Jews by being circumcised and obeying all the details of the Old Testament Law. Paul taught that all that the Gentiles needed to do was to confess their faith in Jesus and follow him for the rest of their lives.

THE COUNCIL OF JERUSALEM

A great meeting of Christians in Jerusalem tried to make it easy for Jewish and Gentile Christians to live together. They told Gentiles in the churches to avoid eating anything offered to idols, or meat that had been strangled or where the blood was left in, and not to commit sexual sin. That way they would avoid publicly embarrassing their Jewish friends. **You can read about this council in Acts chapter 15.**

Did you know?

Groups of believers became known as "the church". In the New Testament, the word "church" means a group of people, not a building. These groups met in homes to worship and to learn about the teaching of Jesus. They were first called "Christians" in Antioch as a nickname. The word is used only three times in the New Testament.

Facts!

There were many good Roman roads between the main cities in Paul's day which made travel fairly easy. The Roman army kept the peace and acted as a police force, so there was less chance of meeting with trouble. People travelled for trade and it helped to be a Roman citizen, which Paul was, even though he was a Jew. On more than one occasion he used this to get out of trouble.

Paul the traveller

Acts 16-18:22

The second missionary journey

Paul was a great traveller. His second missionary journey started off once again at Antioch. This time he travelled with another friend called Silas through what is now southern Turkey. They went back and preached to the churches that they had helped to start on their last visit. In Lystra a young man named Timothy joined them on their travels. When they got to Troas on the north-west coast, Paul had a vision during the night of a man from Macedonia in northern Greece. This man was begging him to come to Macedonia. Paul and his companions set off at once for Greece. This was the first time that the good news about Jesus was taken to people in Europe.

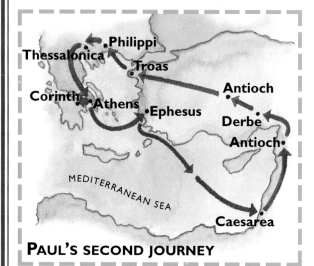

PAUL'S SECOND JOURNEY

Churches in Europe

They travelled through northern Greece, and visited the town of Philippi. A woman called Lydia was the first to believe in

Jesus when Paul preached. Soon there was a group of believers in Philippi. Paul and Silas faced many hardships. They were thrown into prison, beaten up and accused of being trouble-makers. But they kept on preaching about Jesus in the towns of Greece. There were groups of Christians in Berea, Athens and Corinth by the time they set off for home.

A great letter-writer

Wherever he went, Paul preached to people and formed churches. These were often mostly made up of Gentiles who knew very little about God. They needed to learn how to live to please God. Since Paul couldn't always be visiting them, he wrote letters. There are thirteen of Paul's letters in the New Testament. In 51 AD, probably whilst he was in Corinth on his second missionary journey, he had to write two letters to the church in Thessalonica to encourage them and to explain certain things. Later on, around 55 AD, when he was on his third missionary journey, he had to write at least twice to the church in Corinth to sort out the many difficult problems that they were having.

SLAVES AND SECRETARIES

Writing was a slave's job. Paul seems to have had someone write out his letters for him. The slave would sit and write as Paul said what he wanted written down. Sometimes he signed

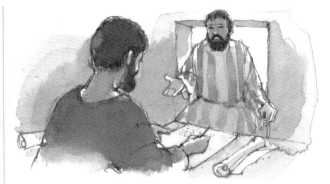

the letter personally to show that it had really come from him. People sometimes call these letters "epistles".

PRISON

Paul had a tough life. Even the churches he had helped to found gave him many difficulties. Perhaps worst of all were the times when Paul was in prison. Imprisonment could be dreadful. Sometimes Paul would be chained and guarded. These prisons were damp, dark and unpleasant places. But in Rome Paul was simply told that he could not leave the house, and he was guarded all the time.

LETTERS TO TIMOTHY

One of Paul's helpers was called Timothy and two of Paul's letters are written to him. They give him advice and encouragement in his life as a young Christian worker. Timothy came from a town called Lystra and had a Greek father and a Jewish mother.

Did you know?

Letters were a very common way to keep in touch. About fourteen thousand letters still exist from the time of the Greeks and Romans. Like today, some letters were very personal, maybe from one friend to another, or from children to their parents. Others were about important matters of government.

Paul's last journeys

Acts 19-28

The "third missionary journey"

At the start of his "third missionary journey", Paul went to Ephesus and stayed there for two years. Ephesus was one of the great cities of the Roman empire. It had a great temple dedicated to the goddess Diana, who is also called Artemis. When Paul preached about worshipping God, the people who made a living by selling statues of Diana started a riot. **Read about this riot in Acts chapter 19, verses 23 to 41.**

A troublesome church

It was during this time that the church in Corinth had big problems. First of all Paul wrote to the Christians there and tried to sort out much of the trouble. They found it very difficult to agree with each other and were doing things that were not Christian. In the end Paul went to visit them again. Whilst he was in Corinth, he wrote perhaps his most famous letter, Romans, to the believers who lived in Rome.

A collection for Jerusalem

Throughout his travels, Paul was very concerned about helping the poor Christians back in Jerusalem. So he spent quite a lot of time encouraging the new churches, which were mostly made up of Gentiles, to give money to a collection for Jerusalem. In 57 AD Paul set off for Jerusalem again to take this gift to them and to prepare for going to Rome later on and perhaps even to Spain.

No welcome in Jerusalem!

Shortly after Paul arrived in Jerusalem he was violently attacked by some Jewish people. They were about to kill him but he was rescued by the Roman army and arrested. Paul was a Roman citizen which meant that he had to be treated with respect. So he escaped being beaten. But it was also decided that he should go to Rome to argue his case. So he was guarded in prison and taken off to Rome where he presented his case to the emperor. On the way to Rome, Paul was caught in a dramatic shipwreck and was nearly killed. **You can read about this in Acts 27 and 28.** The Bible does not tell us what happened to him after this, but some people say that Paul died in Rome.

EPHESUS

Ephesus was a centre of pagan worship especially with its great Temple of Diana. This temple was one of the Seven Wonders of the World, along with the Pyramids in Egypt and the Hanging Gardens of Babylon (see page 67). It is not surprising that Paul faced a lot of evil in Ephesus. But some people who had been practising witchcraft brought their books and burned them in a public bonfire to show that they were now followers of Jesus.

PAUL'S FRIENDS

Paul had many friends who helped him in his missionary work. Barnabas, Timothy and Silas were his main companions on his travels (see pages 94-95). He was also helped by Apollos, a gifted teacher, and

Priscilla and Aquila who ran a business making tents. Paul worked for a time at tentmaking with them. **You can read the names of many of Paul's other friends in Romans 16.**

LETTERS FROM PRISON

Paul used his time in prison to write letters to churches. We can read these letters in the New Testament. His letter to the Philippians is very encouraging. He wrote to the Ephesians and gave them a summary of his main teaching. And he wrote to the church at Colossae (Col-os-y) which he never visited. He wrote a short personal letter to a man called Philemon asking him to accept back his runaway slave. Paul had befriended the slave and he had become a Christian.

A VERSE TO REMEMBER
"Nothing is as wonderful as knowing Christ Jesus my Lord. I have given up everything else and count it all as rubbish. All I want is Christ and to know that I belong to him."
(Philippians chapter 3, verses 8 and 9 CEV)

Other letter writers

Hebrews, Jude, 1,2 and 3 John

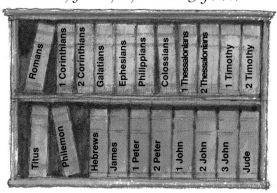

Paul wrote thirteen of the letters of the New Testament, Peter wrote two and James wrote one. The letter to the Hebrews is hardly a letter at all, though it is addressed to a group of Jewish Christians. It is really more like a piece of teaching.

Should we turn back?

Hebrews was written to Jewish Christians who felt tempted to stop being Christians. They were beginning to doubt that Jesus was the Son of God. We don't know who the writer was, but he is very certain that Jesus is really the Son of God. There are many quotes and stories from the Old Testament. In chapter 11 the writer looks back at people in the Old Testament who had faith in God such as Abraham, Moses and many others. The readers are encouraged to stand firm in their faith. **Look up Hebrews chapter 11**. This chapter gives an exciting list of some of the great heroes of the Bible.

The last sacrifice and a new covenant

Hebrews shows how Jesus was the perfect sacrifice for sins (see page 40) so that no sacrifice would ever need to be made again. Hebrews also says that Jesus, through his death, has made a new covenant for his people (see pages 36 and 37). In the light of all this, how could anyone think of turning back from being a follower of Jesus?

Problems in the church

Most of the letters in the New Testament were written to solve problems. John's three letters were written to bring comfort to a group of Christians who had real difficulties. Some people had even left the church. John mentions a man called Diotrephes (Dyo-tre-fees) "who likes to be the number-one leader". But John also writes that it is very important that Christians should love each other. This is what makes them different from people who are not believers. **Look up 1 John chapter 4, verses 7 to 11.**

False teachers

The letter of Jude is not the only place in the New Testament which warns against false teachers who were telling people to believe wrong things. But it does have some very hard words to say about them in verse 16 – "they boast about themselves and flatter others to get what they want."

WRITING MATERIALS

In New Testament times the gospels and letters were written on a scroll made out of papyrus (see page 35), leather or the skin of a young sheep or goat, called parchment. It was usually written in columns on only one side and could be made as long as was necessary by adding on extra lengths or by cutting it. Something more like books began to appear in the second century after Christ. They were called codices. The various leaves were bound together at one edge like books are today.

CHRISTIAN CHURCHES

In New Testament times there were no church buildings or temples as we think of them. People met in homes. So when the Bible mentions a particular church, it means a group of Christians like the Jewish Christians who received the letter to the Hebrews or the Christians in Corinth or Rome who received letters from Paul. Sometimes people today think of the first Christians as belonging to a "perfect" church. This is far from being the truth! Many of the letters in the New Testament were written to sort out dreadful problems.

Did you know?

Many of the first Christians suffered persecution from Jews, Romans and others. They were thrown to lions, crucified and treated in many other cruel ways. Often this was simply because they refused to worship the emperor.

A VERSE TO REMEMBER

"God is love. If we keep on loving others, we will stay united in our hearts with God, and he will stay united with us."
(1 John chapter 4, verse 16 CEV)

The future

Mark 13, the Book of Revelation

War and destruction

Like most people, Jesus' disciples were very interested to know what was going to happen in the future. Jesus taught his disciples about what would happen to them after he had returned to heaven. He warned them about disasters and wars to come and false teachers who would pretend to speak on his behalf. Jesus also told his disciples that the **temple** in Jerusalem would be destroyed. These things all happened during the Jewish War of AD 66 to 70. The Jews tried to rebel against their Roman masters and were severely beaten. The temple in Jerusalem was destroyed and it seemed that the Jews would never again be masters in their own country. What Jesus had warned about, actually happened.

The end of the world

Jesus also taught about the very end of the world when he will return. He told parables to his disciples to teach them that they should always be ready for him to return. He taught them that at the end of time there would be a final judgement when he himself will separate all human beings into two groups - those who believe in him and those who do not. One of the most famous of these parables is about ten bridesmaids. Five of them were ready for the arrival of the groom. Five were not. **You can find these parables in Matthew chapter 25.**

The Book of Revelation

Like the book of Daniel in the Old Testament, the Book of Revelation is a strange kind of book called apocalyptic (apo-ca-lip-tic; see page 69). The writer was called John. He was writing to seven churches in the far west of present-day Turkey. They were experiencing many difficulties. John encouraged the believers by telling them that God would judge the Roman Empire in which they lived. He paints a word-picture of the Roman world collapsing, with its leaders being judged by God. Roman trading ships and wealthy merchants were shown to be cheats. John also had a vision of heaven. He describes the thrilling worship that the believers are enjoying even now in heaven. **Look up Revelation chapters 4 and 5.**

The return of Jesus

Before God finally judges the world, Jesus will return. The book of Revelation describes him as a great conqueror riding on a white horse. He will judge his enemies. **You can read about this in Revelation chapter 19, verses 11 to 21.** Following this, God will judge everyone who has ever lived and create a new heaven and a new earth. The Bible ends with a message of great hope.

PICTURES AND SYMBOLS

The book of Revelation and some of the teaching of Jesus are full of unusual pictures and symbols. Sometimes they are copied from Old Testament books like Daniel. For example, Daniel describes other nations in terms of wild animals like a bear or a leopard. Revelation also uses animals as symbols. On other occasions these pictures are like codes for the Roman empire or for the emperor. The numbers 666 in Revelation chapter 13, verse 18, have caused a lot of interest. When they are translated into Latin they spell out the name Nero, who was a particularly evil Roman emperor.

Facts!

Some Roman emperors

Augustus (Aug-us-tus; BC 27 to AD 14) - emperor when Jesus was born.

Tiberius (Ty-beer-ius); AD 14 to 37) - ruled during the rest of Jesus' life.

Caligula (Cal-ig-yoo-la; AD 37 to 41) - who was mad!

Claudius (Clor-dius; AD 41 to 54) - who had a bad stammer!

Nero (Neer-o; AD 54 to 68) - who set fire to Rome!

Three emperors in one year (AD 68 to 69)!

Vespasian took over (Ves-pay-zyan; AD 69 to 79).

Titus (Ty-tus; AD 79 to 81)

Domitian (Dom-ish-yan; AD 81 to 96) - Revelation may have been written at this time.

A VERSE TO REMEMBER

"Amen! Praise and glory and wisdom and thanks and honour and power and strength be to our God for ever and ever. Amen!"
(Revelation chapter 7, verse 12 NIV)

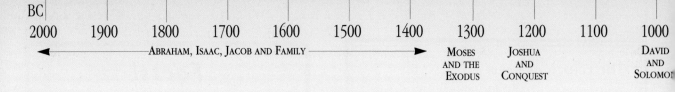

BC										
2000	1900	1800	1700	1600	1500	1400	1300	1200	1100	1000

◄——— ABRAHAM, ISAAC, JACOB AND FAMILY ———►

MOSES AND THE EXODUS

JOSHUA AND CONQUEST

DAVID AND SOLOMON

God's plan for the world

From the old to the new

John the Baptist was a sort of bridge between the Old and the New Testaments. He was like an Old Testament prophet, but prepared the way for Jesus to come. Some people in Israel were ready to hear Jesus' message when he began his ministry. Jesus certainly brought something new. He taught that, in his life and ministry, the Kingdom of God had arrived (see page 78). People needed to get right with God.

God breaks in

In Jesus' miracles, teaching and especially in his death and resurrection, God was breaking into people's lives in a new way. Jesus is the **Messiah** Israel had been waiting for. The four gospels give accounts of Jesus' life and ministry. Jesus left his disciples and went back into heaven. He told them to wait until he had sent them the power of the Holy Spirit and then go and tell the world about him.

Pentecost

Pentecost (or Whitsun) is the birthday of the church. The Holy Spirit was sent from heaven to help the first Christians to know the power and the presence of Jesus in their lives. Thousands of men, women and children became believers in Jesus and their lives were filled with the Holy Spirit.

Paul

Paul was the first great missionary and writer in the early church. He travelled as much as he could in the Roman world of his day to take the message of Jesus to both Jews and Gentiles. He wrote many letters to groups of believers, helping them to understand how to live as followers of Jesus. He taught them about God, the Lord Jesus, worship, personal behaviour and many other things.

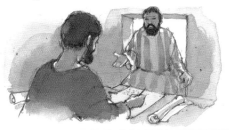

| 900 | 800 | 700 | 600 | 500 | 400 | 300 | 200 | 100 | 0 | 100 | AD |

THE DIVIDED KINGDOM (ISRAEL AND JUDAH) THE FALL OF SAMARIA (722BC) THE FALL OF JERUSALEM (587BC) *EXILE* EZRA AND NEHEMIAH ALEXANDER'S CONQUESTS THE MACCABEAN REVOLT JESUS, PAUL AND THE EARLY CHURCH

From beginning to end

The New Testament lets us know God's plans for the future. We don't know this in detail, but we do know that God, who created the world in the beginning, will be there at the end. He will create a new heaven and earth. And this time there will be no sin to make things go wrong as there was in the Garden of Eden (See page 18).

APOSTLES

The first apostles were the twelve disciples of Jesus. Jesus wanted them to be witnesses of all that he did and said. Most of all they were meant to be witnesses of Jesus' resurrection. Paul is also an apostle because Jesus appeared to him on the road to Damascus and appointed him as apostle to the Gentiles. Sometimes in the New Testament other people are called apostles but in their case it simply means that they were missionaries.

Did you know?

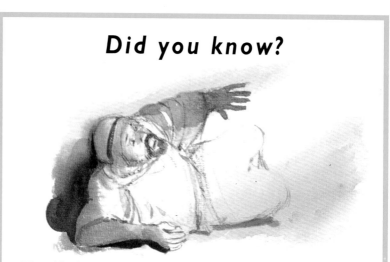

Paul had probably never met Jesus during his life on earth. In his letters, he never describes Jesus and rarely refers to any incidents in Jesus' life. Sometimes he hints at knowing Jesus' teaching. But Paul did know Jesus as his Lord because he had met him after his resurrection. Jesus had spoken to him in a blinding light on the Damascus road. Look up page 94. It was there that Jesus called Paul to be his apostle and the preacher to the Gentiles.

Facts!

Roman rulers tried to stamp out Christianity but, instead, it grew rapidly. Jesus' followers obeyed his command and took his message all over the Roman world. Early in the fourth century the Roman emperor claimed he had become a Christian. Christianity was well on the way to becoming the main religion of the Roman empire.

A VERSE TO REMEMBER

"Long ago in many ways and at many times God's prophets spoke his message to our ancestors. But now at last, God sent his Son to bring his message to us."
(Hebrews chapter 1, verses 1 and 2 CEV).

How we got the Bible

The books of the Bible were written down over a long period of time. Parts may have been written as much as three thousand years ago. Some, of course, were not written until after the time of Jesus. Christians believe that God speaks to us in the Old and New Testaments and that is why the Bible is so important. By the time of Jesus, the books which make up the Old Testament had been written and collected together. By the end of the fourth century AD, the books which are in the New Testament had also been collected together.

Saint Jerome

The church is made up of people from all nations and languages. So it is not surprising that from the very beginning of the history of the church, there were translations of the Bible into languages which people understood. Not everyone could understand Greek and Hebrew, the

languages in which the Bible was first written! The most important early translation was begun by Saint Jerome in Bethlehem in the late fourth century. He translated the Bible into Latin which most people at the time could understand. This version is called the Vulgate.

The Reformation

In the fifteenth and sixteenth century, a movement began which is called the Reformation. It led to a division of the

church into Roman Catholics and Protestants. The protestant reformers believed that it was important that everyone should be able to read the Bible in their own language. By now only learned people could understand Latin. Two men who translated the Bible into English were John Wycliffe and William Tyndale. Tyndale became a martyr for translating the Bible. He was burnt at the stake in 1536, but many other followers continued his work. In 1612 King James the First of England permitted the "Authorised Version" of the Bible to be printed. It is sometimes called the "King James Version". This became the main Bible of the English-speaking world for over three centuries.

The twentieth century

There have been many translations of the Bible in the twentieth century, not only into English but into a great many other languages as well. Today we have a choice of several English translations. The ones used in this book are the Good News Bible (GNB), the New International Version (NIV), and the Contemporary English Version (CEV).

HERE IS JOHN CHAPTER 3, VERSE 16
IN THE THREE VERSIONS.

For God loved the world so much that he gave his only Son, so that everyone who believes in him may not die but have eternal life.
GNB

For God so loved the world that he gave his one and only Son, that whoever believes in him shall not perish but have eternal life.
NIV

God loved the people of the world so much that he gave his only Son, so that everyone who has faith in him will have eternal life and never really die.
CEV

WRITERS

Sometimes we know who wrote the books of the Bible. This is true for a book like Paul's letter to the Romans. But we don't know who wrote all the books. Sometimes they are called after the most important person of the time. For example the first five books of the Old Testament are called the Books of Moses, though it is unlikely that he wrote every part of them. What matters is that the church has understood that God had inspired these books and can still speak through them.

SCROLLS

The first copies of the Bible were scrolls of individual books. The reader had to unroll the text in order to reveal the next column. Soon after the writing of the New Testament, codices (co-dis-ees) were invented (see page 101). They are more like our books today and were much easier to carry around than scrolls.

PRINTING

The invention of the printing press was very important. It made the making of Bibles very easy indeed. Before this time monks had copied the words of the Bible letter by letter. This took a long time. The first important work to come from a printing press was the Gutenberg Bible. It was in the Latin language and was made in 1456 by Johann Gutenberg, who lived at Mainz in Germany.

What the Bible means to us

Pictures of the Bible

The Bible sometimes uses picture-language to describe itself. For example, it is like a light, which shows us the way. Sometimes it is described as "the word of God". It is like honey and refreshes those who read it like drinking water. **Look up Psalm 19 verses 7 to 11.** It warns and guides and changes people's lives. It is the most powerful book in the world and the Christian's greatest possession.

God's great plan

The Bible is all about God. It tells us what he is like, what he has done and what he commands. The Bible tells us how God made the world, people and animals. It is about how those people sinned and did wrong. And it is about what God has done to put things right by sending the Lord Jesus Christ to earth so that we can know God. This is God's great plan.

True stories

The Bible tells us the stories of great and godly people like Abraham, Moses, David, Mary and Paul. **You can read about many others in Hebrews chapter 11.** Most important, it tells us about Jesus. It describes his life, his teaching and how God the Father raised him from the dead. If we did not have the Bible, we would know almost nothing about these people and their lives.

The truth

The Bible is full of wisdom. It teaches us how to please God and how to keep out of trouble. But it also tells us the truth about God and about life. It helps us to understand what kind of person we are and the best way to live. It tells us the truth, yet gives us lots of hope as well. It corrects us and encourages us.

God's guidebook for living

The Bible teaches us God's way of living. If we want to know how to behave or what might be the right thing to do, the Bible will help us to make a decision. This doesn't mean that the Bible is always easy to understand. Sometimes we need to ask advice from other Christians or read books about the Bible. Often God wants us to think very hard about what he says in his word. And that might take some time!

WHERE TO START

It is a good idea to get a modern translation of the Bible, which is easy to understand. See page 107 for more information about these. The best place to start reading the Bible is probably the Gospel of Luke. Luke tells us about the life of Jesus. Some of it will probably be very familiar. When you've read that, look at Luke's book about the early church - Acts. This makes exciting reading. You will read about the people to whom many of the letters of the New Testament were written. You might like to turn to the Book of Psalms in the Old Testament which contains all sorts of prayers and hymns to God.

HOW TO READ THE BIBLE

It is good to read whole books of the Bible through fairly quickly, like you would read a story in an ordinary book. This gives you a good idea of what actually happened. Sometimes we should stop and read a small piece, even just a few verses, and think carefully about them. Whenever we read the Bible, it is important to pray that God will speak to us, because the Bible isn't just any book, but God's word through which he speaks today. There are many magazines and books written to help you use the Bible. Some are available from the publishers of this book.

A VERSE TO REMEMBER
"Your word is a lamp that gives light wherever I walk." (Psalm 119, verse 105 CEV)

Did you know?

The Bible is the world's all-time best-selling book. However, less than a third of the world's six and a half thousand languages have any part of the Bible. Nearly a thousand languages need translation teams. Missionary organisations like Wycliffe Bible Translators are working hard to meet the need.

Time chart for the Old Testament

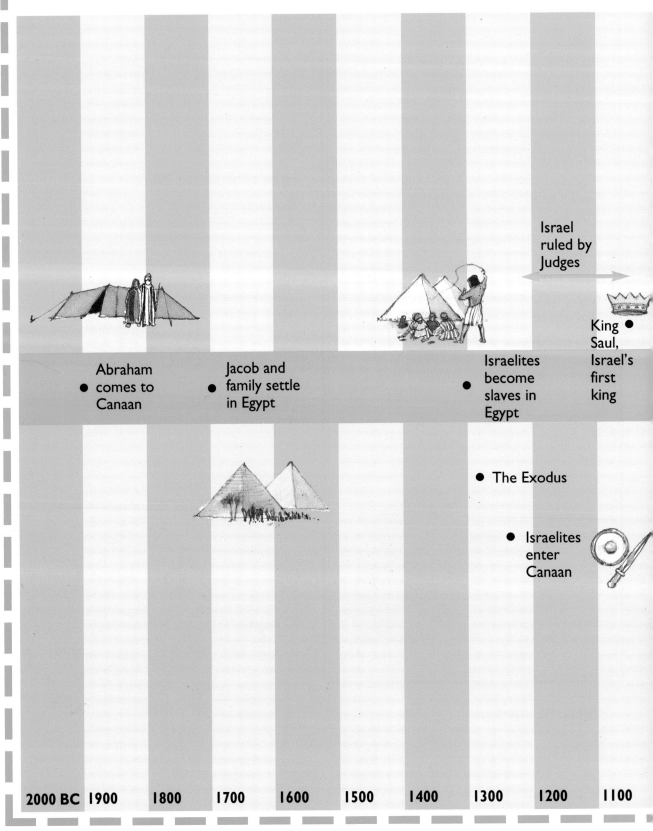

Abraham comes to Canaan

Jacob and family settle in Egypt

Israelites become slaves in Egypt

Israel ruled by Judges

King Saul, Israel's first king

The Exodus

Israelites enter Canaan

2000 BC 1900 1800 1700 1600 1500 1400 1300 1200 1100

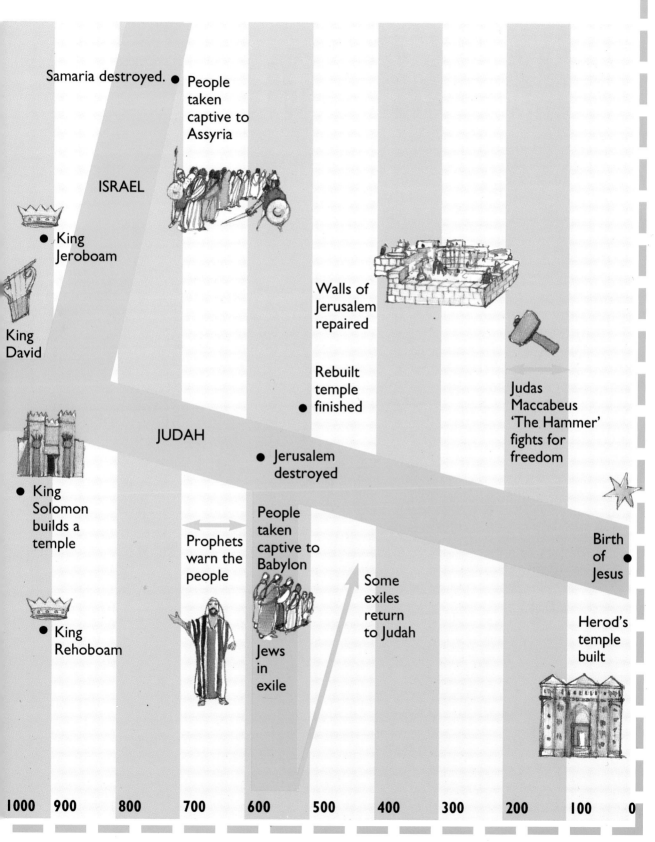

Samaria destroyed. ● People taken captive to Assyria

ISRAEL

● King Jeroboam

King David

Walls of Jerusalem repaired

Rebuilt temple ● finished

Judas Maccabeus 'The Hammer' fights for freedom

JUDAH

● Jerusalem destroyed

● King Solomon builds a temple

Prophets warn the people

People taken captive to Babylon

Some exiles return to Judah

Birth of ● Jesus

● King Rehoboam

Jews in exile

Herod's temple built

| 1000 | 900 | 800 | 700 | 600 | 500 | 400 | 300 | 200 | 100 | 0 |

Time chart for the New Testament

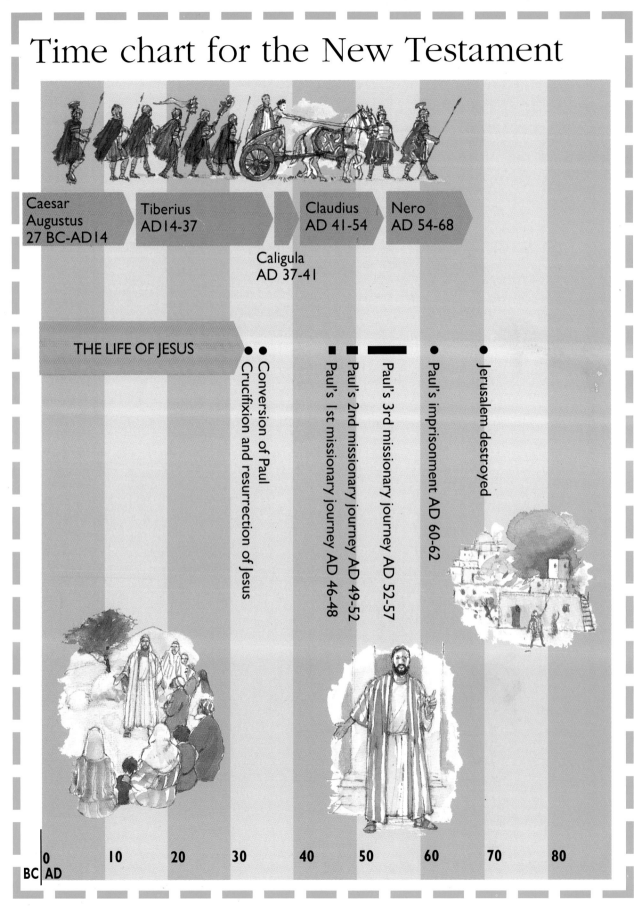

Caesar Augustus 27 BC-AD14

Tiberius AD14-37

Caligula AD 37-41

Claudius AD 41-54

Nero AD 54-68

THE LIFE OF JESUS

Crucifixion and resurrection of Jesus

Conversion of Paul

Paul's 1st missionary journey AD 46-48

Paul's 2nd missionary journey AD 49-52

Paul's 3rd missionary journey AD 52-57

Paul's imprisonment AD 60-62

Jerusalem destroyed

BC | AD

0   10   20   30   40   50   60   70   80

Jerusalem at the time of Jesus

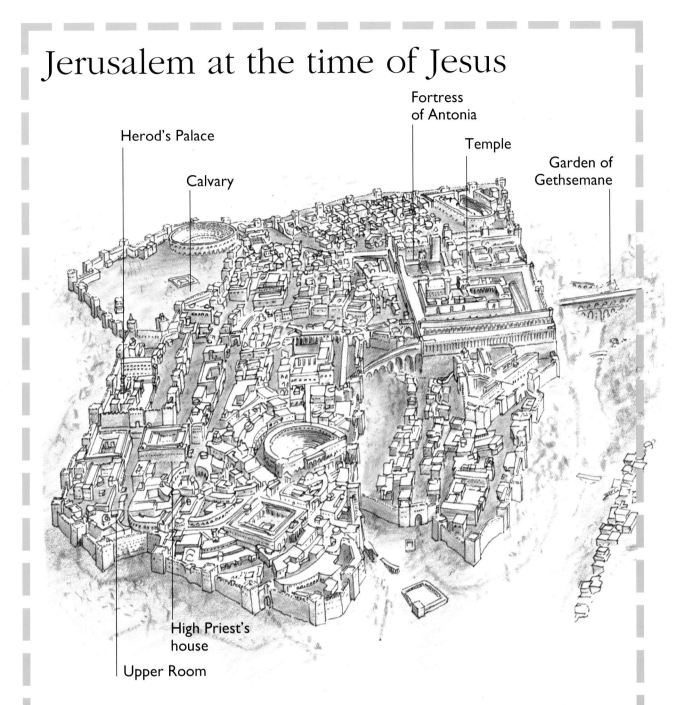

Herod's Palace

Calvary

Fortress of Antonia

Temple

Garden of Gethsemane

High Priest's house

Upper Room

It was King David who made Jerusalem important. The city was built on a hill which made it easier to defend against attackers. So David wanted it to be his capital. You can read about how David captured Jerusalem in 2 Samuel chapters 5 and 6. King Solomon built a temple there and placed the ark of the covenant in it. So Jerusalem became even more important and people came from all over Israel to worship God there at festival times.

In 587 BC the Babylonians destroyed Jerusalem and the Jews went into exile. Seventy years later they began to return and rebuilt the city. It was King Herod who rebuilt the magnificent temple which Jesus visited. But it was destroyed again in 70 AD by the Romans because the Jews had begun a rebellion. Nowadays Jerusalem is still a holy city for Jews, Christians and Moslems. The drawing shows the city at the time of Jesus, though we cannot be certain of the exact location of some places.

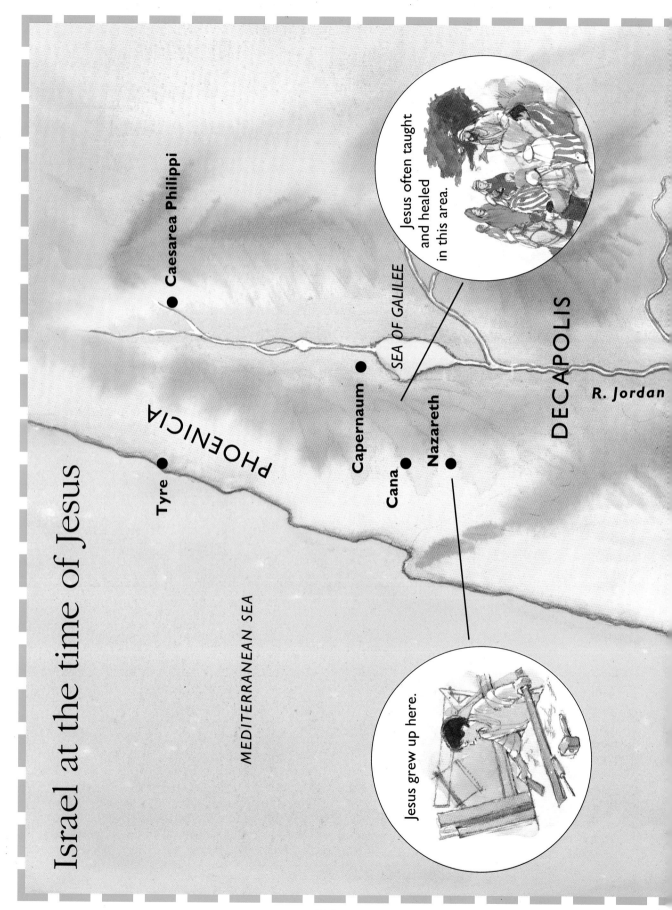

Israel at the time of Jesus

Caesarea Philippi

Tyre

PHOENICIA

Capernaum

Cana

Nazareth

SEA OF GALILEE

DECAPOLIS

R. Jordan

MEDITERRANEAN SEA

Jesus often taught and healed in this area.

Jesus grew up here.

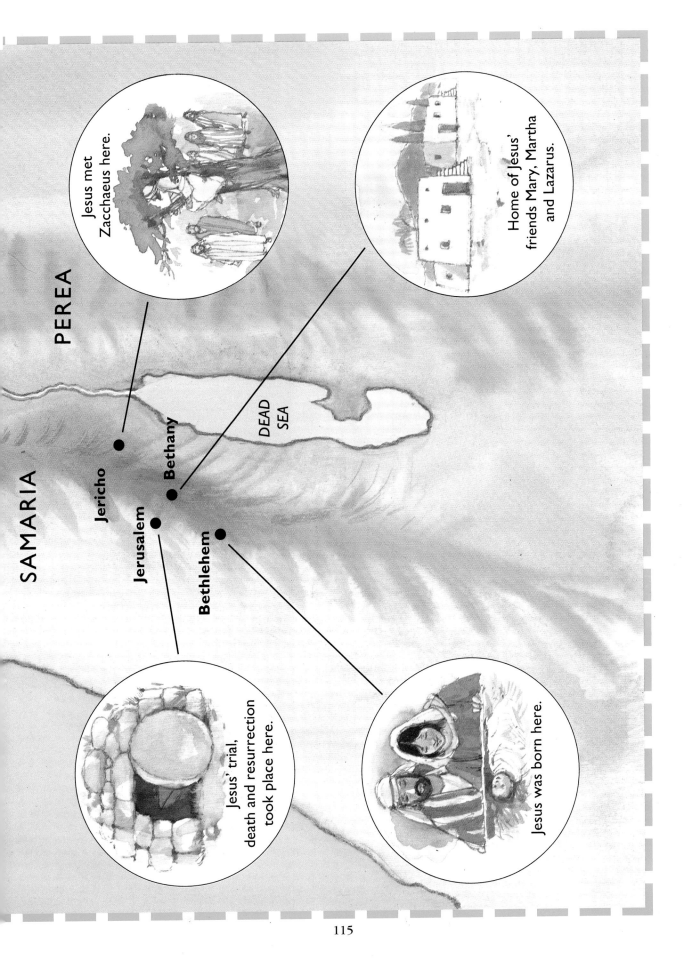

PEREA

SAMARIA

Jericho

Bethany

Jerusalem

Bethlehem

DEAD
SEA

Jesus met
Zacchaeus here.

Home of Jesus'
friends Mary, Martha
and Lazarus.

Jesus' trial,
death and resurrection
took place here.

Jesus was born here.

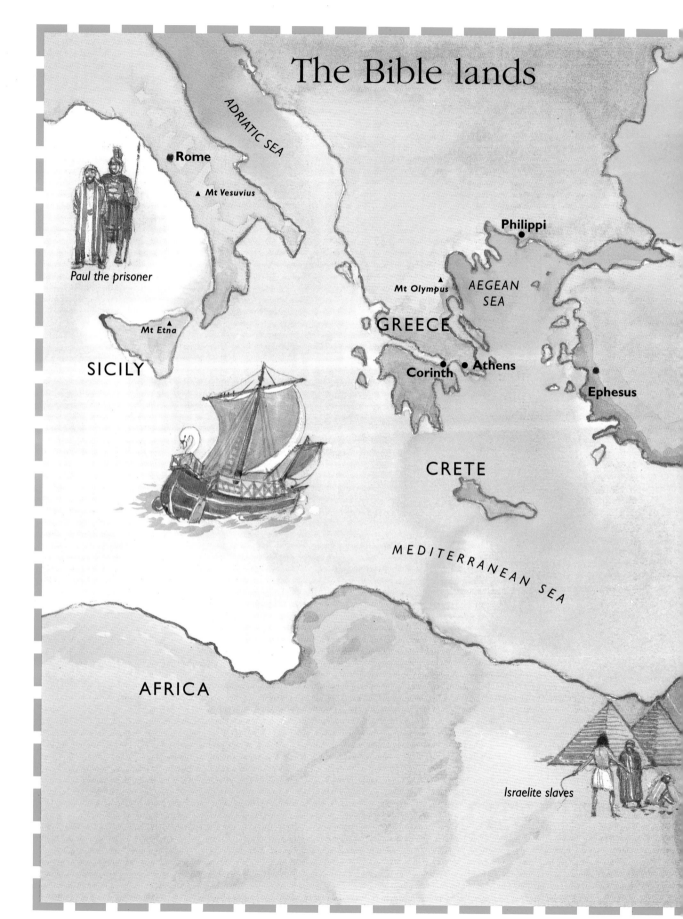

The Bible lands

ADRIATIC SEA

● Rome

▲ Mt Vesuvius

Paul the prisoner

▲ Mt Etna

SICILY

Philippi ●

Mt Olympus ▲

AEGEAN SEA

GREECE

Corinth ● ● Athens

● Ephesus

CRETE

MEDITERRANEAN SEA

AFRICA

Israelite slaves

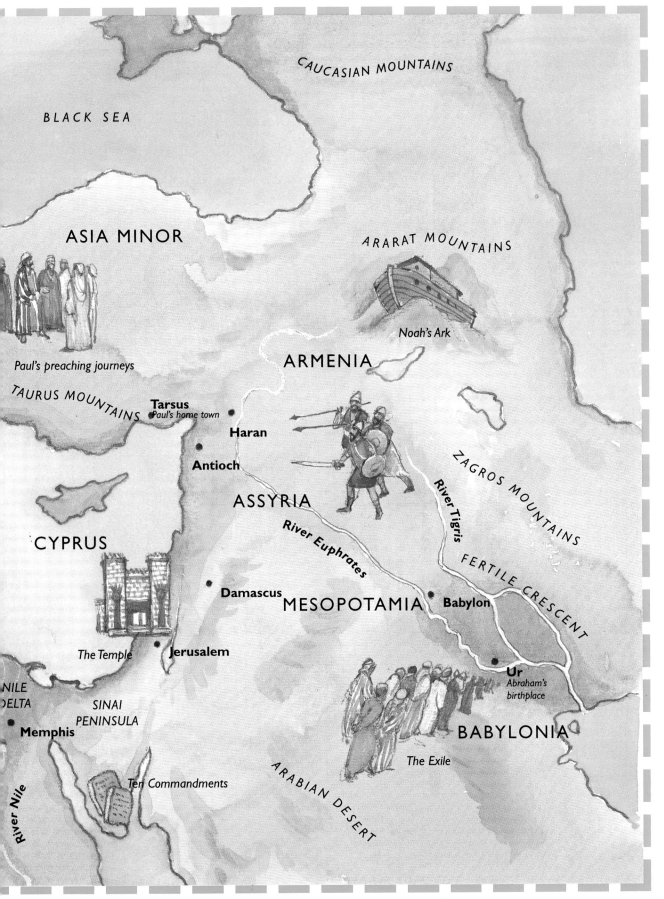

BLACK SEA

CAUCASIAN MOUNTAINS

ASIA MINOR

ARARAT MOUNTAINS

Noah's Ark

ARMENIA

Paul's preaching journeys

TAURUS MOUNTAINS

Tarsus
Paul's home town

Haran

Antioch

ASSYRIA

ZAGROS MOUNTAINS

River Tigris

River Euphrates

FERTILE CRESCENT

CYPRUS

Damascus

MESOPOTAMIA

Babylon

The Temple

Jerusalem

Ur
Abraham's birthplace

NILE
DELTA

SINAI
PENINSULA

Memphis

BABYLONIA

The Exile

Ten Commandments

ARABIAN DESERT

River Nile

Who's Who?
A guide to people in the Bible

Names are sometimes very important in the Bible.
For example, God changed Abram's name to Abraham. Saul's
name was changed to Paul when he became a follower of Jesus.
For more about names, see page 31.

Aaron – the elder brother of Moses who was chosen by God as the first High Priest. See page 41.

Abel – the second son of Adam and Eve who was killed by his brother Cain. See page 18.

Abram/Abraham – called "the friend of God". He and his wife Sarah were called by God to be the parents of the Israelite people. See pages 22 and 23.

Absalom – one of King David's sons who started a rebellion against his father. See page 53.

Adam – the first man Adam and his wife Eve were also the first people to commit sin. See pages 18 and 19.

Ahab – a wicked king of Israel who, with his Canaanite wife Jezebel, were enemies of Elijah. See page 58.

Barnabas – a companion of Paul on his first missionary journey. See page 94.

Bathsheba – the wife of Uriah whom King David had killed. Then David took her as his own wife. See page 53.

Cornelius – the first Gentile to become a Christian. See page 92.

Daniel – a Jewish exile in Babylon who remained true to God at all times. See pages 68 and 69.

David – the shepherd boy who became the second and most famous king of Israel. See pages 48 to 53.

Elijah – one of the first and greatest prophets in Israel who challenged the prophets of Baal on Mount Carmel. See pages 58 and 59.

Elisha – the follower and successor of Elijah. See pages 58 and 59.

Esau – the son of Abraham and twin brother of Jacob who cheated him out of his birthright. See pages 24 and 25.

Esther – a Jewish woman who became the queen of King Artaxerxes in Persia and was able to help her people. See page 69.

Gideon – one of the judges who led the Israelites against the Midianites. See pages 44 and 45.

Isaac – the son of Abraham who married Rebekah and received the promise. See pages 24 and 25.

Isaiah – one of the greatest prophets of the Old Testament. See pages 62 and 63.

Jacob – the twin brother of Esau and son of Isaac. His twelve sons were the founders of the twelve tribes of the Israelites. See pages 24 to 27.

Jeremiah – a great Old Testament prophet who predicted that the Israelites would be sent into exile. See page 66.

John – the brother of James. They were called "sons of thunder" by Jesus and became his disciples. See page 77.

John the Baptist - the cousin of Jesus who prepared the way for him by preaching to the people. See pages 74 and 75.

Jonah – an Old Testament prophet who was swallowed by a large fish. See page 57.

Jonathan – the son of King Saul and friend of David. See pages 49 and 50.

Joseph – one of the twelve sons of Jacob who was sold into slavery by his brothers but became very successful. See pages 28 and 29.

Joshua – the friend and successor of Moses who took the Israelites into the Promised Land. See pages 42 and 43.

Judas Iscariot – the disciple who betrayed Jesus. See page 84.

Laban – Jacob's uncle and the father of Rachel. See page 26.

Lazarus – the brother of Mary and Martha in Bethany whom Jesus brought back from the dead. See page 80.

Lot – Abraham's nephew who escaped from Sodom. See pages 22 and 23.

Luke – the travelling companion of Paul who wrote a gospel and the book of Acts. See pages 88 and 89.

Mark – the cousin of Barnabas and companion of Paul after whom one of the gospels is named. See page 88.

Mary – the wife of Joseph and mother of Jesus. See pages 76 and 77.

Matthew – a disciple of Jesus after whom one of the gospels is named. See page 88.

Miriam – the sister of Aaron and Moses. See page 34.

Moses – the great leader of the Israelites who brought them out of Egypt to the borders of the Promised Land. See pages 32 to 41.

Naaman – a Syrian army commander who was cured of leprosy. See pages 58 and 59.

Naomi – the mother-in-law of Ruth, who returned to Israel from Moab after a famine. See pages 46 and 47.

Nebuchadnezzar – a king of Babylon who destroyed Jerusalem and led the people off into exile. See pages 66 to 69.

Nehemiah – a Jewish official in the Persian empire who led some of the Jews back to Jerusalem and rebuilt the city walls. See pages 70 to 71.

Nicodemus – a Pharisee who came to Jesus at night to talk to him. See page 83.

Noah – the man who built the ark when God decided to destroy the world in a flood. See page 20.

Paul – the great apostle and missionary who wrote many New Testament letters. See pages 94 to 99.

Peter – the brother of Andrew and leader of Jesus' disciples. See pages 77, 84, 92 and 93.

Pontius Pilate – the Roman leader who condemned Jesus to death. See page 84.

Ruth – the Moabite daughter-in-law of Naomi who returned with her to Israel and married Boaz. See pages 46 and 47.

Samson – the Israelite leader who fought against the Philistines. He married Delilah who betrayed him. See page 44.

Samuel – the last of the judges who prepared the way for the Israelites' first king, Saul. See pages 48 to 50.

Saul – the first Old Testament king. See pages 48 to 50.

Shem – one of the sons of Noah and brother of Ham and Japheth. See page 20.

Solomon – David's son, the very powerful third king of Israel. See pages 54 to 55.

Stephen – an early follower of Jesus, the first person known to have been killed for his faith. See page 92.

Timothy – a young travelling companion of Paul, who became a church leader. See pages 96 and 97.

Important words in the Bible

Ark of the covenant – a special box which was kept in the most holy place in the tabernacle and, later on, in the temple. See pages 40, 48 and 52.

Blasphemy – making insulting or incorrect statements about God. See page 84.

Blessing – a strong way of promising some good gift. See page 22.

Covenant – a special agreement usually between God and certain people. See pages 21 and 23.

Devil – God's chief enemy. He is sometimes called Satan. See page 76.

Exile – being sent far away from your home country. See page 62.

Holy Spirit – the powerful presence of God on earth. See page 93.

Idols – false gods, often statues made out of wood or metal. See pages 36 and 56.

Israelites – God's special people in the Old Testament. Sometimes called Hebrews or Jews. See page 32.

The Law – God's special rules given to the Israelites on Mount Sinai. See page 32.

Messiah (or Christ) – the leader expected by the Jews in the Old Testament. The New Testament describes Jesus as the Messiah (or Christ). See pages, 74, 80 and 104.

Most holy place – Part of the tabernacle and temple where only the High Priest was allowed to enter once a year. See page 55.

Promised Land – the land of Israel which God promised to the Israelites in the Old Testament. See page 22.

Sabbath – the name of the Jewish holy day. See page 40.

Sacrifice – an offering to God of an animal, bird or food. See pages 23 and 40.

Scripture – the Bible, God's special book. See page 66.

Sin – doing anything which displeases God. See page 18.

Slave – a person who is bought and forced to work. See page 28.

Synagogue – the building where Jews worship, both at the time of Jesus and today. See pages 66 and 72.

Tabernacle – the large tent in which the Israelites worshipped before the temple was built in Jerusalem. See pages 30, 33 and 40.

Tax collectors – much hated men who collected money for the Roman government in the time of Jesus. See page 82.

Temple – the large place of worship built in Jerusalem by Solomon and rebuilt after the exile. See pages 30, 55, 70 and 102.

Tribe – a large extended family. The Israelites had twelve tribes descended from the sons of Jacob. See page 30.

Index